THE COUNTER REFORMATION

The Counter Reformation

G. W. SEARLE M.A.

ROWMAN AND LITTLEFIELD
Totowa, New Jersey

First published in the United States 1974
by Rowman and Littlefield, Totowa, N.J.

2>0·6
Se17

200157

ISBN 0 87471 528 8
ISBN 0 87471 529 6 Paperback

Printed in Great Britain

CONTENTS

INTRODUCTION THE DECLINE OF THE
MIDDLE AGES   7

PART I THE MEDIEVAL CHURCH   11
1. The Papacy: the Seeds of Decay   2. The Personnel
3. Theology and Doctrine   4. The Church and Society
Principal Events

PART II THE CHURCH CHALLENGED:
EARLY REFORM AND PROTESTS   29
5. The Growth of Criticism   6. The Forces of Revival
7. Reform Frustrated, the Failure of Leadership   Principal
Events

PART III SIXTEENTH-CENTURY REFORM BEFORE
TRENT, THE MOVEMENT GATHERS PACE   55
8. The Challenge of Luther   9. The New Orders   10. Reform
outside Italy: Princes and Individuals   11. The Papacy, the
Revival of Leadership   Principal Events

PART IV THE COUNCIL OF TRENT   81
12. The First Session   13. The Second Session and the
Achievement of Paul IV: *Paul IV*   14. The Third Session
and the Significance of the Council   Principal Events

PART V THE REFORMED PAPACY   99
15. The Triumph of Leadership: *Reform in Italy–
Administrative reforms*   Principal Events

PART VI THE COUNTER REFORMATION IN
ACTION   113
16. Western Europe   17. The Struggle for Central Europe
18. Success and Failure in the North   19. The Final Success
Principal Events

CONCLUSIONS **165**

APPENDIX I THE POPES OF THE LATE
MEDIEVAL AND EARLY MODERN PERIOD **177**

APPENDIX II THE SECULAR RULERS **178**

APPENDIX III GENEALOGICAL TABLES **180**

APPENDIX IV BIBLIOGRAPHY **182**

Index **185**

MAPS

The Religions of Europe *c.* 1570 **110**
The Religions of Europe 1648 **111**
Central Europe **141**

INTRODUCTION
The Decline of the Middle Ages

The idea of a Counter Reformation originated in the work of the nineteenth century German historian, Ranke. Although many of his contemporaries, such as von Pastor and Maurenbrecker, doubted whether the Catholic revival was essentially a reaction to Protestantism, the notion has lingered on and twentieth-century historians, notably Jedin and Evennett, have continued to debate the subject; few writers would now accept that it was primarily brought about by the Protestant Reformation, but considerable discussion remains on its origins and timing, Spain, Italy and the Netherlands all being suggested as starting points.

Although there had been reforming movements throughout the Church's history, those of the sixteenth century produced changes on a greater scale than before; this was largely because the fifteenth and sixteenth centuries were a period when the social, political and intellectual structure of medieval Europe was questioned and often successfully overthrown. Since the Church was inherently a part of medieval society, it was also forced to respond to those challenges. Thus, primarily, the Counter Reformation was a readjustment by the Catholic Church to meet the changing conditions of the early modern period and, as such, although profoundly affected by Protestantism, it ran parallel to the Protestant Reformation.

To many Europeans, the late fifteenth and early sixteenth century was a period of depression, when the future looked bleak and uncertain, yet the challenges which presented themselves were to revitalise western Europe. By the early years of the sixteenth Century, the rise of nation states with strong

monarchies had delivered some shattering blows to the concept
of a united Christendom, and Francis I's alliance with the Turks
in the 1530s proved to be more typical of the age than Charles
V's last attempt at a united Christian crusade. Princes increasingly became masters of their own domains, at the expense
of free towns, cities, parliaments, feudal aristocracy and of the
Church itself; definite theories of royal absolutism appeared in
France, where the Pragmatic Sanction of Bourges (1438),
amended by the Concordat of Bologna (1516), gave the Crown
a large measure of temporal power over the Church. The Valois
were certainly no longer merely the feudal kings of Paris.
Geographically modern France had taken shape.

This pattern was repeated in England where the Wars of the
Roses destroyed traditional political obligations, and where
Edward IV and Henry VII ruled because they had won the
struggle for power; nor were they under the necessityof consulting
groups or institutions, with the result that Parliament and the
Church became very much royal instruments. Henry VII's son,
guided by Thomas Cromwell, not merely invoked the 1351–93
Statutes of Provisors and Praemunire but carried through a
Reformation which made the King Supreme Head of the English
Church and also supreme over all his territories.

The same trend occurred in Spain where the union of Aragon
and Castile, and the expulsion of the Moors from Granada in
1492, gave a new found vigour and at least the appearance of
unity under royal leadership. Lack of an effective central
authority allowed the princes of Italy and Germany to extend
their control over their own princedoms, and Lutheranism
appeared as a heaven-sent gift to aid the latter. Even as far
afield as Russia, Ivan III attempted similar processes while the
Scandinavian monarchs followed suit, especially in Sweden
after the establishment of the Vasa dynasty.

None of this should be exaggerated, however. Much of the
political unity was superficial, much of the law and order only
wishful thinking; nevertheless the unity of Christendom was
broken, in theory as well as in practice. The disputes between
pope and individual monarchs had gone decisively in favour of

the latter; the medieval arguments of Marsilio of Padua, John of Paris and William of Occam proved more suited to fifteenth and sixteenth-century conditions than those of the papal supporters Giles of Rome and St Thomas Aquinas.

Although the Italian Renaissance initially affected only an intellectual minority it ultimately influenced the educated classes of the whole of western Europe. Based upon the revival of classical literature, the movement diverted interest away from the saints and the after-life to the life of action upon earth and to the activities of man. The visual arts and the literature of the period paid homage to the dignity and to the unlimited potential of man, which in turn helped to stimulate a growth in lay education, by no means confined to Italy. Books were written, by Castiglione on the way to behave as a courtier and by Machiavelli on the policy to be pursued by a prince, which gave little attention to Christian morality; new areas of thought were explored in medicine, mathematics and philosophy. Meanwhile in astronomy Copernicus produced a heliocentric theory of the universe which not only challenged the concepts of medieval astronomers but also the ideas of Christian theologians – furthermore the discovery of printing ensured that such information would be circulated and would endure.

The medieval Church had often frowned upon the business life, yet as the commerce of Italy, south Germany and the Netherlands expanded in the late fifteenth and sixteenth centuries so capitalist enterprise also intensified. Elsewhere urban communities began to grow on the new trade routes, especially those with ready access to the Atlantic, but, while these produced excellent vehicles for the interchange of ideas, they often further alienated men's minds from the teachings of the medieval Church.

Moreover the latter years of the fifteenth century and the whole of the sixteenth century saw an almost continuous rise in prices and population, and as the feudal systems of Europe faltered under these stresses, changes in land tenure occurred. Anabaptism, the Knights' and Peasants' Revolts in Germany and the Pilgrimage of Grace and Ket's Rebellion in England were indications of deep strains in society; those possessing land, or renting it upon defined and suitable terms, who could produce and sell, and those who traded in others' goods cashed in on a rising market, but the future was bleak for those with questionable deeds to their land, and for labourers and peasants as a whole. Thus there arose an explosive atmosphere in which people of the lower orders were open to exploitation by demagogues with revolutionary ideas and so, to the intellectual dissatisfaction of the educated laity was added popular discontent, often on the verge of open revolt.

An entirely new factor stimulated the life of Europe in the fifteenth and sixteenth centuries – increased contact with the outside world. The sinister threat of the Moslem Turk in southeast Europe and the Mediterranean was significant, but more important were the overseas discoveries. As the Portuguese drove around Africa to India and the Far East, and the Spanish reached and opened up Central and Southern America, so astronomy, navigational methods and instruments, geography, the treatment of native populations and the use or misuse of vast quantities of precious metals, became important issues. Ultimately the New Worlds altered the political balance of Europe by enhancing the importance of those countries with Atlantic seaboards, and the immediate future rested with Spain, Portugal, France, the Netherlands and England.

Such changes inevitably forced the Roman Catholic Church into a reassessment of its doctrine and of its position within society.

PART 1
The Medieval Church

[1] THE PAPACY: THE SEEDS OF DECAY

It is easy to dwell upon the obvious abuses of the medieval
Church, as if they were the root causes of discontent, and therefore of both the Reformation and Counter Reformation.
Pluralism, absenteeism, nepotism, clerical ignorance and im-
morality certainly existed, but they were by no means new; the
Church had not suddenly grown corrupt, and contemporaries,
on the whole, accepted abuses, if such they were, as arrangements necessary for carrying on the Church's work. Uneducated
clergy were better than no clergy at all, and when clerical
incomes were reduced to as little as £5 p.a. pluralism was often
the only method by which a priest could have any sort of
living. Such corruption is therefore not necessarily a true
indication of the condition of the Church, and a closer look at its
institutions may reveal less obvious, but far more serious
weaknesses.

From the eleventh century the popes made a determined
effort to establish their control over the Church and their
spiritual superiority over secular princes, writers such as Giles
of Rome (1247–1316) and popes such as Gregory VII (1073–85),
Innocent III (1198–1216) and Boniface VIII (1294–1303)
making what might seem outrageous claims for papal authority.
Basing much of their argument upon precedent they claimed
that Charlemagne had accepted that the spiritual sword was
superior to the temporal; similarly they attempted to show
through the 'Donation of Constantine' that the Emperor

Constantine had transferred certain rights over the western Empire to the Papacy, and it was not until the fifteenth century that the philologist, Lorenzo Valla, proved the document to be a forgery.

The peak of papal power came during the pontificate of Innocent III; an interdict was placed over the English Church and King John excommunicated after a quarrel concerning the appointment of Stephen Langton to the see of Canterbury; Philip II of France was humiliated after an unlawful divorce, while throughout these quarrels Innocent interfered decisively in German affairs and succeeded in forging useful links with the new universities. Despite this, the highest statement of papal pretensions appeared a century later during the quarrel between Boniface VIII and Philip IV (1285–1314) of France. John of Paris, in defence of the king, had argued that the prince's authority derived directly from God, thus denying the right of the Papacy to interfere in temporal matters; in reply, Boniface published, in 1302, the bull, *Unam Sanctam*

For by the witness of truth the power spiritual must institute the power temporal and must judge it if it be not good. . . . Therefore if the temporal power errs it shall be judged by the power spiritual. . . . This authority, though it be given to a man and exercised by a man, is not human but rather divine, granted by God's word to Peter, confirmed to him and his successors in whom Christ called the rock. . . . In consequence of which we declare, assert, define and pronounce that it is entirely necessary for salvation that all human creation be subject to the Pope of Rome.

Nevertheless, despite the claims of Innocent IV (1243–54), the secular princes generally gained ground, a process accentuated by the papal residence at Avignon between 1309 and 1379.

In 1305 Clement V, a Frenchman, was elected Pope. Inheriting the increasing difficulties in administering the Papal States, he moved to Avignon, which was then just outside the Kingdom of France. This placed him very much under the political influence of the French Crown, and in the eyes of Europe the idea of the Papacy as an independent arbiter and agent of God's will lost ground. Furthermore, the papal administration strained every effort, while at Avignon, to increase its financial resources, towards the day when a return to Rome would be possible; its income became three times greater than that of the Crown of France, but many of the methods of raising money were bitterly resented. The sale of indulgences and pardons, the practice of retaining the income of vacant benefices and the demands for annates and Peter's Pence rapidly increased the feeling that the Papacy had become primarily concerned with raising money.

A yet greater loss of independence and prestige was caused by the Great Schism from 1378–1417. Blessed with sufficient cash, Gregory XI, himself a Frenchman, returned to Rome in 1378 where he died, whereupon Urban VI was elected. Although Italian, it was considered that he would be acceptable to the French but this unstable man proved acceptable to very few people, with the result that a number of cardinals withdrew from Rome and elected a rival Pope in Clement VII, a Frenchman, who promptly returned to Avignon. At the Council of Pisa in 1409 a third Pope was elected whom it was hoped most would accept. Most did, but not the supporters of either the Rome or Avignon claimants; the Schism therefore dragged on until a compromise was reached in 1417 at the Council of Constance when Martin V was elected. To safeguard his position Martin was forced to make concordats with the princes of western Europe, by which they were granted considerable rights over the Churches in their states, a far cry from the great days of Innocent III and the claims of Boniface VIII.

Not only were papal claims to superiority over the secular princes finally set aside, but the Councils which brought the Schism to an end challenged the authority of the Papacy within the Church itself. The movement which advocated conciliar supremacy will be discussed in the next chapter and it is sufficient here to notice that, throughout the fifteenth century, the popes fought against such ideas and, although largely victorious by 1500, the memory of the struggle lingered on and explains the Papacy's reluctance to summon further Councils.

Throughout all its troubles the late medieval Papacy contrived to build the most efficient administration in the western

world. During the pontificate of Innocent III a determined
effort was made to organise more efficiently the Papal Curia,
(the collective name given to the governmental departments,
the administrators and the papal entourage) which the Avignon
residence, far from interrupting, speeded up by the accumulation
of new sources of wealth.

The department of Chancery developed as it organised and
recorded papal correspondence, including the issuing of bulls,
while the growth in the income of the Papacy produced a
corresponding development in the Treasury. In the Consistory
pope and cardinals joined together in what was the highest
assembly of the Church's administration; here new cardinals
were elected and appeals were heard from other papal law courts
and from the individual states of Europe.

In this, the cardinals played an important, if at times a
reluctant part; resentful of the pope's power they frequently
made agreements prior to papal elections that whoever of their
number was elected should increase the cardinals' authority
at the expense of his own. Successive popes, however, chose to
forget their pre-election promises. Nevertheless, certain powers
were confirmed to the cardinals, the most important being their
sole right of electing each pope, which was first formally granted
in 1059. During the latter half of the fifteenth century, however,
after the failure of the Conciliar Movement, the cardinals increasingly became papal agents and their struggle for independent
power was lost. Although many remained the agents of their
national governments and never even visited Rome, as in
Wolsey's case, the pope more than balanced this by the appointment of Italian supporters and, where necessary, of his own
relatives; such a practice was often the pope's safeguard against
a hostile array of cardinals particularly, when, late in the
fifteenth century, the Curia was divided by the family feuds of
Rome. Significantly, from 1471 onwards the cardinals became
more and more Italian, as did the Papacy itself, Adrian VI
(1522–23) from Utrecht being the last non-Italian to hold office.

Thus during the fifteenth century when the Papacy lost ground
to the European princes it established its authority over the

institutions of the Church, and this was also true of its position within the Papal States, which were even enlarged under Alexander VI (1492–1503) and Julius II (1503–13) by the conquest of the Romagna and Bologna. With little shortage of money, and attracting to itself some of the ablest Italians, the unruly city of Rome was brought under control and partially rebuilt, and an efficient administration created which was much admired by foreign observers; at the same time, the popes took their places as leading patrons of the Italian Renaissance. Since the popes of the late fifteenth and early sixteenth centuries who achieved this were, like Alexander and Julius, primarily worldly men, leading their family factions in the politics of Rome, they considerably lowered the spiritual reputation of the Papacy but, on the other hand, they succeeded in creating a firm base in central Italy.

[2] THE PERSONNEL

Spread throughout Europe were approximately 700 bishops and archbishops of whom 277 were in Italy, 118 in France, 65 in the Empire, 57 in Spain and Portugal and 21 in England. To regard them as the agents of the Papacy is to see a situation which Gregory VII or Innocent III hoped to create, but which never came about; except in Italy the Papacy was never able to control their appointment and, despite many bitter quarrels, the prince himself came to appoint and use his bishops as royal agents. There were exceptions, like Becket and Anselm, who saw the pope, not the king, as their direct master, but Wolsey was much more typical, and if the pope wished to have serious representation within the princes' courts, only a resident ambassador or a specially appointed legate could be relied upon.

The bishops held sway, not only within their national churches but also as feudal overlords and as political advisers. In times when lay education was at a premium only the Church could provide men of ability who were essential to the civil government, and certainly not before the sixteenth century could secular rulers do without their help. This often led to the appointment to high church office of men noted for their administrative rather than their spiritual qualities, and their continued presence at court led them to be absentees. When Carlo Borromeo took up residence as Archbishop of Milan in 1565, he was the first archbishop to live there for more than a century; ascetics like Ximenes of Toledo and Fisher of Rochester were the exceptions. In certain parts of Europe, Germany in particular, these bishops had even become princes in their own right.

One third of Germany was in the hands of prince bishops, amongst the greatest of whom were the Archbishops of Mainz, Trier and Cologne who were three of the seven princes entitled, by the Golden Bull of 1356, to elect the Holy Roman Emperor. In some cases bishoprics could be and were actually bought and kept in the hands of a particular family, and it was partly against such a practice that Luther protested in 1517, when Tetzel was raising money, through the sale of indulgences, to recoup some of the outlay which the Elector of Brandenburg had recently made in buying the archbishopric of Mainz. Similarly bishoprics were given away as bribes or as rewards in the diplomatic and political game; in this manner Wolsey received the sees of York, Lincoln, Tournai, Bath and Wells, Durham and Winchester. Moreover, in some cases, the recipient of such a title whether by gift or purchase, was not even ordained, and occasionally, had not even reached the age of discretion. But these were the faults of the late medieval Church in general, and the bishops at the end of the fifteenth century were little worse than in preceding centuries and, in regard to the standard of their education, they were probably better.

Bishops could, either directly or through appointed officials, run their dioceses much as they wished. Their greatest power, and the one which came to be most resented, lay in their law courts which had jurisdiction not merely over the clergy, and spiritual matters, but also over moral offences including matrimonial affairs, testaments and wills. Although a layman might be tried in the Church court, it was not normally permissible for a cleric to appear before the lay magistrate, a point which laymen quickly appreciated and resented. By the fifteenth and sixteenth centuries the Church's administration of justice was amongst its most unpopular aspects and led to legal and popular opposition as in the case of Richard Hunne, in 1515, in London.

So much of the bishop's time was devoted to the service of the state or the business of administering extensive lands, that little was left either for the close supervision of the ordinary clergy, or for their own participation in pastoral duties. It was not that the majority were not able men, nor that they were more self seeking and corrupted than other great landlords or officers of state; it was simply that most had lost touch with ordinary lay people, and equally important, with the lower ranks of the clergy.

The ordinary clergy of medieval Europe varied enormously in their wealth, their position and the standard of their education. Few received a university education although, with the founding of new universities in the fifteenth century there was an improvement, but those who had, were earmarked for administrative jobs in and around the cathedral. These, however, were in the minority. The majority toiled with little understanding and with little hope of reward. Their incomes derived from the parish tithes and from the endowment left by the original builder of the church, but usually this went to the rector, perhaps a layman, a university or a local monastery who employed the vicar. Salaries were consequently low, going down to as little as £5 p.a. in early sixteenth-century England.

If the level of education of these men was low so, by necessity, was the standard of instruction which they passed on. Few understood the Latin of the service, and in any case, it was believed that the more repetition of masses reduced one's time in purgatory. Sermons were rarely preached and it is significant that the reformers of sixteenth-century Europe, as the friars before them, placed great emphasis on the spoken word of instruction.

The local priest was hardly distinguishable from his parishioners and many carried this similarity even further by being secretly or openly married, although the actual percentage is still disputed; for all this it would be wrong generally to condemn the parish clergy of Europe. It was not that standards were worse than at earlier periods but that by the fifteenth and sixteenth centuries laymen were in a better position to point an accusing finger. Furthermore, it would be unfair to ignore the fact that the bulk of the lower clergy carried on their day to day ministering as best they could, and it is perhaps significant that the parish parson is one of the few churchmen to be treated favourably by Chaucer. Nevertheless, it was unavoidable that more and more attention would be focused on the inadequacies of the parish clergy. Furthermore these underprivileged lower ranks of the Church themselves often resented their position and contrasted it with that of the wealth and importance of the upper ranks of the hierarchy; when the Church was attacked they often joined in, following perhaps the millenary preachers of Germany, the Anabaptists or other radical leaders. Thus the loyalty of large numbers of the lower clergy was one of the great problems confronting the medieval Church.

The lower clergy disliked those other bulwarks of the medieval Church, the orders of monks and friars, especially since many clerical livings were actually controlled by the monasteries. The ideal of the life of prayer and meditation, withdrawn from the world was older than Christianity itself, but its practice in Europe dated probably from the Benedictine monasteries of the sixth century. Within the Benedictines various groups arose, and later other orders were founded separately, the most important of which were the Carthusians in 1084 and the Cistercians in 1100. From these orders there sprang others, particularly those founded on military lines and connected with the reconquest of the Holy Land, such as the Knights Templar and the Teutonic Knights of the early twelfth century.

Through generous benefactions the monasteries acquired great wealth and became, after the princes themselves, the greatest landowners of western Europe; to such an extent was this so that their dissolution in many countries at the time of the Reformation resulted in a complete revolution in land ownership. Most orders saw their heyday in the thirteenth century; the remains of high Gothic buildings, such as Fountains, Rievaulx and Tintern in England, pay tribute to their power and wealth, but, by the late fourteenth and fifteenth centuries the great fervour of monasticism was on the decline; perhaps wealth and power produced lives that were too comfortable, perhaps power itself corrupted but certainly widespread evidence told of debauchery at worst, and inattention to spiritual matters at best. It is true, that much of the evidence was consciously hostile, as in the reports on the English monasteries prepared for Thomas Cromwell in the 1530s. It is true also that innumerable communities continued their lives in a blameless way; nevertheless the monastic ideal became unfashionable and writers as different as Boccaccio and Erasmus attacked them.

For some, the monkish life was too withdrawn and as the monasteries became bound up with wealth and power, there arose groups who challenged both monasteries and parish priests. These were the mendicant orders of friars of which the first were the followers of St Francis of Assisi. The Franciscans or Grey Friars, founded in 1210, were followed by the Dominicans or Black Friars in 1215, the Carmelites or White Friars in 1245 and the Austin or Augustinian Friars in 1256.

Friars opted to work within the world and not to live in withdrawn communities, thus their foundations appeared particularly in the towns of the thirteenth and fourteenth centuries where they came to do the work which the ordinary parish clergy would not or, more usually, could not do. They aimed to preach and minister and to carry Christian charity to the poor and needy, and they in no way felt restricted by the presence in a town of a parish church, nor by another order and everywhere they sprang up side by side. With their power of preaching direct to the masses, their impact on society was explosive and they became one of the greatest influences on late medieval life.

Although initially pledged to poverty, gifts and endowments inevitably poured in, and the Franciscans in particular found themselves embarrassed to such an extent that the order split more than once between those who would, and those who would not accept, that the order should possess property. Before long, the orders of friars, like the monastic orders, grew powerful, and by the fifteenth century they were linked, in the eyes of the laity, with the established order of society.

Nevertheless, the friars produced some of the greatest minds of the late middle ages, notably St Thomas Aquinas and William of Occam, and they did much to inject vitality into the whole Church. Moreover, although the orders became closely connected with the universities, they retained their links with the towns and with common people – to the continuing anger of the established church. This rivalry between parish clergy and friars ultimately weakened the Church, as did the rivalry amongst the friars themselves which ranged from academic, theological arguments to disputes over the possession of land.

Although the friars escaped the barrage of criticism levelled at the monasteries, their practice seems to have weakened with the passage of time; their ideals, however, did not, and by the fifteenth and early sixteenth centuries they were reappearing, throughout Europe, in societies dedicated to working within the world.

[3] THEOLOGY AND DOCTRINE

The most important figure in the formulation of the theology of the medieval Church was the Dominican friar, St Thomas Aquinas (1226–74). Not all his contemporaries accepted his work in full, but later writers have seen his teaching as the pinnacle of medieval thought. Broadly known as Scholasticism, and often as Thomism, it derived from traditional Christian writing and from Aristotle whose works, rediscovered in the twelfth century, made a deep impression on European intellectual developments after Aquinas had fused them with Christian thought.

Aquinas argued that man could attain knowledge only through the use of reason based upon the experience of his senses; neither faith nor divine illumination alone could instil knowledge and even the existence of God could not be accepted purely as a matter of faith. From the Aristotelian concept of a completely orderly and symmetrical universe he deduced the existence of God as the all powerful prime mover, upon whom man was, at all times, dependent; hence reason and faith were separated although Aquinas believed that reason would serve to substantiate faith and never to contradict it.

Although he accepted that there were certain points of the Christian faith, such as the Incarnation, which were beyond man's reason, Thomism was a philosophy in which reason and the intellect were exalted and it soon came to dominate the universities of Paris, Oxford and Cambridge. The belief that knowledge was to be acquired by the application of reason to Christian dogma unfortunately led ultimately to over-subtle academic argument upon abstruse parts of the faith, and many felt that this was not only unprofitable, but was at the expense of true religion, to such an extent that during the fourteenth century a large degree of scepticism arose amongst theologians.

Aquinas's ideas dislodged, but never destroyed, the older ideas of the Augustinians who took the existence of God as their starting point and attributed all true knowledge to divine illumination. In this system, reason and faith were one, since faith and illumination led directly to man's ability to use his reason. Augustinianism, with many variations, continued to find exponents and to exist side by side in the medieval Church with Thomism.

Amongst the points of doctrine which were later disputed it was generally accepted that there were seven sacraments ordained by God: baptism, penance, marriage, the ordination of priests, the eucharist (celebration of the mass), confirmation and divine unction (the last rites). Within the mass it was believed that, at the blessing of the wine and the bread, transubstantiation or a physical change took place wherein the bread and the wine actually became Christ's body and blood. Hence at each celebration, Christ was sacrificed again to atone for man's sins, and the altar therefore was of great significance in

Catholic churches. The laity received only the bread and few would actually partake more than once a year. Nevertheless mass would be said on all special days in the calendar, and in general the medieval Church placed greater emphasis on its sacraments than on its pastoral work.

At high levels within the Church there were those who accepted some degree of predestination, but the orthodox believed that man was justified in the eyes of God partially through his own actions (though whether these were carried out through his own or through a God-given strength was hotly disputed) and partially through God's grace. Thus there was something which man could do to secure his after life and this bait was a necessary component of the ordered medieval society. To offend against society or its established government could thus be equated with sin.

There were those who suggested that ultimate authority in matters of doctrine and teaching rested only within the revèaled words of the Scriptures but this was generally not accepted; the orthodox view being that authority rested with a combination of the Scriptures, the evolved body of canon law and with the official *ex Cathedra* statements of the pope. Even were a layman sufficiently educated to study the Bible, his interpretations would still have to conform to Church pronouncements and the medieval Church repeatedly asserted that it, and it alone, was the interpreter of spiritual matters. Printing, translations of the Bible and increasing lay education were thus to pose great problems in the late fifteenth and early sixteenth centuries.

The practice of confession also placed the Church in a strong position within society; since the clergy had the right to hear the confessions of the laity and to name penances which must be done in order to obtain absolution, the priest obtained an intimate knowledge of his parish. In theory, at least, this gave him a superiority over the laity, yet many of the clergy were hardly distinguishable from their parishioners. Nevertheless the teaching that absolution could only be gained through the mediation of the Church remained.

[4] THE CHURCH AND SOCIETY

A new problem arose in the fourteenth and fifteenth centuries when the merchants of northern Italy, southern Germany and the Netherlands and other commercial centres accumulated considerable wealth. The Church never officially sanctioned the accumulation of capital, and although by no means practising such restraint itself, it held to the New Testament doctrine that no man should exploit another. It has often been suggested that it was dislike of this doctrine which helped convert business people to Protestantism, but this is most unlikely since neither Luther nor Calvin sanctioned capitalist practices any more than did the Roman Church itself; nevertheless the relevant fact in the late Middle Ages was that the Church condemned the practice of usury without being able to stop it, and this was at a time when the classical revival of the Renaissance glorified the life of action and human success.

The classical revival also pointed the way to new scientific ideas and here again traditional philosophy proved obstructive; little free discussion was possible in an age when the Church was not only the sole repository of learning but also the judge of intellectual morality. All fields of science suffered from its deadening hand, but none more so than astronomy and medicine. The Church, basing its ideas on those of the second-century mathemetician and astronomer, Ptolemy, taught that the earth was the centre of the universe and that God had made all other heavenly bodies revolve around it; to challenge such an idea was therefore heretical, especially since it might lead to a questioning of the Church's central position upon earth. To study and dissect the human body was considered sacrilegious, and progress in medicine was therefore impeded. Although not all medieval Christians followed the Church's teachings on medicine, astronomy and the other sciences, to oppose them was difficult and true intellectual freedom did not exist.

There was then considerable divergence of opinion on main issues of doctrine and belief, and to establish strict orthodoxy

would not only involve great difficulty, but possibly the aliena-
tion of large sections of the Church itself. At the highest academic levels these differences suggest a doctrine so clouded as
to ensure continuing disputes, while at the lowest levels there
was too little understanding of the Church's teaching and too
much emphasis on the almost superstitious worship of saints and
relics, and on the prospect of the fiery torments of hell.

It is even arguable that, to the ordinary and superstitious mind
of the later Middle Ages, Christ was no longer the focal point of
the Christian religion. Pilgrimages to the shrines of well-known
saints were important events in the calendar, and each individual or parish might well direct their particular prayers to a
special saint, especially to the Virgin Mary, while the possession
of relics, such as a splinter from the cross, a thorn from Christ's
crown or a bone from the skeleton of a saint, was felt to be most
effective in gaining answers to prayers.

Worse still was the growing practice of selling indulgences.
The prospect of purgatory and hell was close and very terrible,
and the Church, in its quest for money, was quick to realise this
potential; by buying an indulgence the purchaser acquired some
of the surplus goodness of the saints and so shortened his stay in
purgatory, which was that state in which the soul was purged of
its earthly sins. It was, in fact, against such practices that
Luther protested in 1517 when Leo X issued a proclamation
which entitled indulgences to be sold in Brandenburg

We do herewith proclaim that our most holy Lord Leo X, by divine
providence present Pontiff, has given and bestowed to all Christian
believers of either sex who lend their helpful hand for the recon-
struction of the cathedral church of St Peter, the Prince of the
Apostles, in Rome, complete indulgence as well as other graces and
freedoms, which the Christian believer may obtain according to the
apostolic letter dealing with this matter.

Whether people still realised that they were worshipping and
praying to Christ through an intermediary is unclear; but undoubtedly one of the major failings of the medieval Church was
the lack of concentration on Christ and his teachings, and it was

precisely this fault which reformers of all shades of opinion were to point out in the sixteenth century.

Nevertheless, in many ways the greatest weakness of the Church was caused by its own success. As its bishops obtained wealth and position, as the monasteries accumulated land and feudal power and as the friars spread amongst the population, so the Church became identified with the established order of the state; its leaders were no longer seen in spiritual or in pastoral terms and they came to represent the authoritarian aspect of medieval society which became so much resented. Immune from civil jurisdiction yet sitting in judgement over the laity, the hierarchy resembled judges rather than Christ's disciples. The wealth of the Church, and above all, the diverse methods of raising money accentuated its acquisitive nature and increased opposition to the privileges which the clergy enjoyed; consequently it seemed that the Church's principal concern was the preservation of an established social order in which its own position was secure. There is, therefore, little wonder that the laity and poor clergy combined in peasants' revolt to denounce secular government and Church hierarchy in the same breath.

Yet the Church's position was self-perpetuating since it attracted the ablest men and trained them for its service. This, however, was changing as the standard of lay education improved. Moreover, as control of the national Churches passed into the hands of the princes during the fifteenth century, so reform, of whatever kind was deemed necessary, could come only with government approval and direction; ultimately therefore, the Church, by becoming so much an instrument within the state, weakened its ability to deal with its own abuses.

In any case the Church's attitude to its own reforming and revivalist movements changed rapidly in the late Middle Ages. Between the eighth and twelfth centuries the western Church was fairly free of heresies or, at least, it managed to absorb movements which might have become heretical; from the twelfth century onward, however, the record of heresy is almost continuous and, although numerous shades of opinion still existed,

it became more difficult for new movements to remain within
the main body of the Church.

The ambitions of the great popes of the twelfth and thirteenth
centuries led to a search for orthodoxy and uniformity which
was increased as the Church's prestige declined during the
Captivity and Schism. In defence of its authority the Church
rejected movements which seemed likely to challenge its
doctrine or structure; those groups already within the Church it
was generally forced to accept and Thomists and Augustinians,
friars and monks continued to live inside the Church, although
often in mutual discord. But new movements could be dealt with
more effectively, and this the Church attempted to do. Consequently many reforming groups of the fourteenth and fifteenth
centuries were forced into becoming heretical movements, and
in the process the Church lost much that was liveliest and most
invigorating in the religious life of the western world.

To reformers therefore the Church appeared even more
conservative, if not actually reactionary, and since this brought
into focus all its other faults and failings so it lost the respect of
the very people who should have been its greatest supporters.
The readiness with which men flocked to the Lutheran, the
Calvinist, the Anabaptist and the revived Catholic orders is
proof of the religious fervour of the age; able and conscientious
men like More and Erasmus and the German theologians Eck
and Cochlaeus lived, hoping for reform, but stifled by the lack of
interest of the Church's leaders.

This was not the whole story, for reform did come, but only
very slowly, and it came most easily in countries like Spain for
quite specific and untypical reasons.

Principal Events

The Papacy at the peak of its ambitions
1073–85. Gregory VII (Hildebrand)
1198–1216. Innocent III
1243–54.　　Innocent IV
1294–1303. Boniface VIII

Foundation of new orders of monks
1084.　　　Carthusians
1100.　　　Cistercians

Foundation of the friars' orders
1210.　　　Franciscans (Grey Friars)
1215.　　　Dominicans (Black Friars)
1245.　　　Carmelites (White Friars)
1256.　　　Augustinians (sometimes called Austin Friars)

1226–74.　　Life of St Thomas Aquinas
1309–79.　　Papal residence at Avignon
1378–1417. The Great Schism

PART II

The Church Challenged: Early Reform and Protests

[5] THE GROWTH OF CRITICISM

Although William of Occam (1300–49) and Marsilio of Padua (1270–1342) aroused little popular excitement, their work did much to prepare the way for the reform movements inside and outside the Catholic Church in the fifteenth and sixteenth centuries. By breaking with traditional scholasticism Occam, in particular, exerted considerable influence upon Luther's early thought and upon the ideas of the sixteenth-century Christian humanists.

Occam, an English Franciscan at Oxford, argued that since God was all-powerful man could not, for certain, predict his action and attitudes; to be able to do so would be, by implication, to accept that there was some limitation on God's freedom of action. To believe, therefore, that all theology was open to man through reason, as St Thomas Aquinas had taught, was to lead man to a dead end. For this reason, Occam placed more emphasis on a study of the divinely inspired scriptures. There, and through prayer, man could gain concrete evidence of what God taught and it should, therefore, be his duty to study and follow it. This being the case, the established Church with its dogma and its self-appointed discipline became less important and Occam began to attack the temporal supremacy of the Papacy, for which he was excommunicated by John XXII. As Occam's beliefs, known as Nominalism or the *Via Moderna*, gained acceptance in the universities, so they led to a much more positive attitude towards religion, and in particular towards Christ and his teaching.

Occam preached the independence of kingly authority against the Papacy, but his work was generally not as politically inclined as that of his Italian counterpart, Marsilio of Padua, who lived much of his working life in Germany – both men, in fact, for a time, served Lewis of Bavaria when he was elected Holy Roman Emperor.

Marsilio accepted that matters of faith were not open to man's reason, but he was particularly concerned with the position of the Church within the state, seeing it as a department within and under the civil government, subject to its laws and its rules. These views, expressed in the *Defensor Pacis* of 1324, later proved so acceptable in Tudor England, that Thomas Cromwell had them translated in order to prove that the Reformation had justification in the past. Marsilio attacked the Church hierarchy and held that the clergy's duty was to understand religion and to teach it; he wanted more study of, and reliance on God's word as revealed in the Bible, and he reacted against the wealth of the Church by preaching clerical poverty. He also attacked the papal supremacy and was one of the growing body of opinion which regarded a General Council as the supreme authority within the Church.

Marsilio and Occam therefore led important attacks on the medieval Church and, although they were not the only fourteenth-century writers to hold such views, their influence in the universities and with secular rulers was of the greatest importance and their lines of attack were soon taken up by others. The struggle between Occam's *Via Moderna* and traditional thought was hard fought in the universities and, although scholastic thought was never extinguished, by the fifteenth century the more critical and empirical ideas of Occam had generally triumphed and, ultimately, this helped to persuade the Church to place teaching before argument.

More popular movements were instigated by John Wyclif

(1320–84) in England and John Huss (1369–1415) in Bohemia.
Many people argue that these movements were not in the direct
line of the Counter Reformation; that, instead, they led more
directly to the Protestant schism, but it is untrue to suggest
that, in the century before Luther, there were ideas and movements which inevitably were to split the Church. Although
there are definite threads running through the ideas of Wyclif,
Huss and Luther none of them originally intended to split the
Church. They were in the same tradition as other reformers and
the difference lies in the fact that, when the Church refused to
broaden its base or compromise, they crossed the line of accepta-
bility, whereas others, for one reason or another, stopped short
of it.

John Wyclif was an Oxford don, whose reforming views
brought him to the notice of Richard II's uncle, John of Gaunt, in
the early 1370s. Gaunt patronised Wyclif in order to formulate
his own views against papal power in England, and, in this way,
Wyclif became a person of great influence, at first within the
train of Gaunt, and then from about 1378 to 1384 in his own
right. Despite intermittent differences upon such matters as
appeals to Rome and papal taxation, the English Crown and the
Papacy usually maintained a successful working agreement in
the fourteenth century and there is little evidence to suggest
that, at the time of Wyclif's writing, there was a real possibility
of a break. There was, however, continual manoeuvring, and
Wyclif was useful in the interplay between Crown and Papacy.

Occasionally even advocating clerical poverty, Wyclif consistently held that lordship and the possession of property were
justifiable only as long as neither was misused. Since the 1370s
was the period of the Avignon Captivity and the Schism, it was
not difficult to make out a case for papal abuse of its property
and position, and the papal right to tax the English Church, to
appoint to certain English livings and to hear appeals from
England could therefore easily be questioned. It was not dis-
similar to the argument used in 1536 to dissolve and appropriate
the monasteries and, even in the late fourteenth century, it was
by no means a useless threat.

Wyclif opposed the whole hierarchical structure of the Catholic Church; he saw no validity for this or for coercive powers; he denied the papal supremacy and he accepted the king as God's vice-regent on earth, without the need for the established Church as an intermediary.

Like his contemporary, Chaucer, Wyclif reserved his particular wrath for the monks, the friars – 'a good friar is as rare as a phoenix' – and the hangers-on of the Church, whom he attacked for their corruption, their lives of luxury and indolence, but, above all, for their refusal to follow the teachings of Christ. Like Occam, Wyclif taught that the Scriptures, which were the concrete evidence of Christ's message, should be studied carefully and acted upon, and, for this reason, the Bible was translated into English and great emphasis placed upon preaching.

He denied the validity of confessions and pardons, believing that God alone could forgive sins and, like many revolutionaries, he looked back in time for his ideal. He sought the purity and simplicity of the early Church, which he contrasted with the lavish establishment of his own time.

As long as Gaunt patronised Wyclif, there was a chance that his voice might produce a national movement, but, by the end of his life, such movement as there had been was doomed to failure. Lollardy continued to exist into the sixteenth century, and it may, to some extent, have helped to ease the path of the Henrician Reformation, but it failed to penetrate the higher reaches of society and so lacked powerful patronage. Wyclif's preachers influenced a number of gentry, but Lollardy became predominantly the religion of the poor, whose survival depended upon secrecy especially after the 1401 statute, *De heretico comburendo* which was specifically enacted against it.

Wyclif himself, was never excommunicated although many of his beliefs were condemned by the Papacy at the Council of Constance in 1415. None of these failures, however, should obscure the importance of Wyclif's ideas, for they were re-echoed throughout Europe in the century and a half following his death and were quickly taken up by the Czech reformer, John Huss.

There was nothing sudden about the outburst of religious feeling stimulated by John Huss in Bohemia in the first decades of the fifteenth century; for years a desire had existed for a more pastoral, evangelical religion, and, to this end, the Bethlehem Chapel had been established by certain citizens in Prague in 1391. It was as rector of the Bethlehem Chapel that Huss made his mark. It is not fair to call Huss simply a disciple of Wyclif; he certainly knew of Wyclif's ideas, for they were translated into the Bohemian language in 1403, and he moved closer to Wyclif as his thought developed but his emphasis was rather different.

They were on common ground in their denial of papal supremacy, neither man seeing justification for this in the Scriptures, and the depths to which the Papacy had sunk confirmed them in their views. Above all, however, Huss wanted the Christian teaching taken to ordinary people, and he therefore laid great emphasis on the Scriptures. Not much interested in academic debate, and seeing the importance of the spoken word in an age when most people were illiterate, he taught his followers to study the Bible and then to go out and preach; in this his views were basically evangelical.

Like many others, he pointed out the abuses of the Church, but on such doctrinal issues as transubstantiation in the mass, he remained orthodox. Only in his denial of the papal supremacy was Huss clearly heretical, and in this he was by no means alone in the early fifteenth century, indeed many high ranking members of the Church adopted an extremely ambiguous position on this subject at the Council of Constance. His views chiefly alarmed those who feared that he might be about to preach some kind of social revolution or some doctrine which would lay so much stress on the individual that the power of the clergy would automatically be reduced. On the other hand, to many, Huss became a national hero.

As always, racial feeling was an important factor in Bohemian politics and since Huss seemed to be preaching against external interference from Rome, and incidentally from Germany too, he came to represent all that was Bohemian and national. For this reason, he obtained princely and popular support. Conversely, the Roman Church saw him as a dangerous threat to its position in Bohemia, and after he had written his major work, *de Ecclesia* in 1412–13, he was summoned to the Council of Constance to explain his views. The Council condemned Wyclif's works and declared Huss a heretic, despite the irony that his greatest heresy was to deny the papal supremacy, which the Council itself was discussing at that same time. In spite of the safe conduct accorded Huss, he was taken and burned in Constance in 1415 on the Council's orders. This act made him a nationalist martyr in Bohemia, and provided a lesson which Luther and the German princes remembered well at the Diet of Worms in 1521.

The execution of Huss created more problems than it solved. Bohemia, already in a state of unrest, soon burst into open revolt in his name. The revolt was partly directed against foreign interference, whether Roman or German, and was partly a social rising against lay and clerical landlords. Genuinely democratic elements were released and communist and anarchist groups appeared; despite these variations of opinion, there were basically two groups within the Hussite movement after Huss's death.

The moderates (Utraquists) laid stress on the obligation of all to take communion in both kinds, whereas, the more revolutionary group (Taborites) denied five of the Catholic sacraments, accepting only baptism and communion as being instituted by Christ himself.

The uprising spread throughout Bohemia, but it soon fell into the hands of the gentry and leading townsfolk who controlled the national assembly, which took to itself the right to govern and regulate the Bohemian Church, and in 1420 the rebels, for a while united, drew up a statement of their aims in the Four Articles of Prague. The Word of God was to be preached freely and communion was to be administered to the laity in both kinds; the Church was to forfeit its ownership of worldly goods and mortal sins were condemned and punishments drawn up.

As a result Martin V declared a crusade against the Bohemian heretics in 1420 and war continued with the divisions amongst the Hussites becoming even more marked, as Utraquists and Taborites fought each other vigorously. During the 1430s matters became more settled. The moderate Utraquists defeated the Taborites and between 1433 and 1436 drew up the Compactata with the Catholic Church which lasted until 1620 when the Hapsburgs were at last in a position to impose the strict orthodoxy of the Counter Reformation. By the Compactata, the Church of Rome lost almost all its power in Bohemia and Utraquism became the accepted creed. The Taborites lingered on, more commonly known as the Bohemian or Moravian Brethren and were still to be found in south-east Europe until the nineteenth century, when many emigrated to the United States of America.

Huss, therefore, brought about the most successful protest against the Catholic Church in late medieval Europe, and helped to establish not merely religious, but also a degree of political, independence such as many rulers were seeking.

As early as 1170, Peter Waldo, a rich Lyons merchant, had founded a lay order whose members gave up their personal property, held goods in common and concentrated on preaching and ministering to the poor. Despite persecution, this group survived in Savoy and Piedmont and in the fifteenth century served as yet another reminder to thinking people of the inadequacies of the established Church. Known as the Waldensians or the Vaudois, many of its members later became absorbed into the Calvinist or Zwinglian movements.

In the writings of Occam and Marsilio and in the popular movements of Wyclif and Huss there was common opposition to papal supremacy. This is not surprising in the light of the Schism and the Captivity, and a greater study of the Scriptures seemed to reveal that there was no justification for the papal claims; to many, the supremacy appeared the result of political manoeuvres dating back, in particular to Hildebrand, Gregory VII, in the eleventh century. Moreover, in late thirteenth and early fourteenth century Europe political trends towards some form of contitutional rule arose, and both the English Parliament and the French Estates General gained aspirations of a more permanent position while, as has been seen, the Bohemian Estates played a vital role in the Hussite revolt.

In these circumstances, therefore, a movement appeared within the Church which held that supreme authority lay, not in the Papacy, but in the General Council. By 1409, even the most fervent supporters of the Papacy were compelled to admit that the only means of ending the Schism was by summoning a General Council, yet by this acceptance alone, the implication of conciliar supremacy was established. The Council of Pisa, which met in 1409, to elect Alexander V, declared that another Council should be summoned in three years time to reform the Church. Alexander V, however, became merely the third claimant to the Papacy, and when the Council of Constance met between 1414 and 1418 its primary task was still to heal the Schism, although many of the delegates remembered that they had also assembled to reform the Church.

There were devout men at Constance, and within all the Councils of the fifteenth century, who struggled hard to produce reform; that they failed to do so, was a tragedy for the Catholic Church, for had they succeeded the upheaval of the Protestant Reformation might have been avoided. Arguments arose almost immediately at Constance over whether reform or the election of a new pope should come first. Many delegates realised that, since the popes' relationship to the Church was the outstanding issue of reform, any pope elected prior to the passing of some restraint upon his power, might dissolve the Council and prevent further discussion.

In order to prevent this, the decree *Sacrosancta* was passed in 1415.

This holy Council of Constance . . . declares, first that it is lawfully assembled in the Holy Spirit, that it constitutes a General Council, representing the Catholic Church, and that therefore it has its authority immediately from Christ; and that all men, of every rank and condition, including the Pope himself, is bound to obey it in matters concerning the Faith, the abolition of the Schism, and the reformation of the Church of God in its head and members.

Further divisions existed, however, because the delegates

were organised by nations and national differences proved an impediment to progress.

France and England were actually at war and this was mirrored in the discussions, moreover the Spanish delegates opposed the idea that reform must precede the election. Nevertheless the key to the whole situation was the underlying desire for a restoration of Church unity and, to obtain this, the parties, in the end, were prepared to compromise, with the result that those who wanted reform first were unable to achieve it.

By 1417 a compromise was reached. A new pope was to be elected, but he was not to be allowed to dissolve the Council until some reforms had been passed. In addition, the decree *Frequens* was enacted which stated that councils were to be held at about ten year intervals and that the pope and cardinals could shorten, but not lengthen, the period of time. Arrangements were made to deal with a crisis such as the one which had produced the Schism in 1378, and so, the Church was given a written constitution, although whether future popes would abide by it was quite another matter.

In 1417 Cardinal Colonna was elected pope as Martin V, and his general acceptance ended the Schism. Minor reforms were passed in 1418 and concordats were arranged between the Church and the nations of Europe. The concordats were important since they gave to the secular princes of Germany, France and England concessions over the papal right to hear appeals, to take annates and to grant dispensations and indulgences, and although in the long run they may not have proved very effective, they satisfied the princes who were thereby less likely to support reforming or anti-papal movements in their own countries. These concordats, together with the minor reforms, were accepted as sufficient and the Council was dissolved in 1418. The question of papal or conciliar supremacy was not resolved, however, and remained a major issue.

In accordance with the decree *Frequens*, another Council was summoned to Pavia in 1423; it later moved to Siena, but achieved little through poor attendance and through the unwillingness of any major prince to take a particular interest.

Consequently, it broke up in 1425, having named Basle as the next meeting place.

By the time the Council met at Basle in 1431, disputes between Pope Eugenius IV and the conciliarists had reached an advanced stage, and the main result of this Council was the failure of the conciliar movement. Eugenius introduced, but was persuaded to withdraw, a bull which would have made the doctrine of conciliar supremacy heresy. In the face of this, the Council counter-attacked between 1433 and 1435, attempting to deprive the pope of certain sources of income by the suppression of annates, reservations and provisions. Eugenius carried out reform within the Papal Curia, and enhanced the stature of the Papacy by the 1436 agreement with the Bohemians but, still more, in the same year, by opening negotiations with the Greek Orthodox Church for reunion. Elated by these successes, in 1437 Eugenius decided on a trial of strength and ordered the Council to move from Basle to Ferrara, in Italy. The issue of supremacy was finally at stake.

Many senior prelates obeyed, and although the ardent conciliarists remained at Basle, their support dwindled. In 1439 they declared conciliar supremacy to be an article of faith, they deposed Eugenius and elected in his stead Felix V. None of this succeeded. The transference of the papal Council from Ferrara to Florence in 1439 and to Rome in 1443 was in itself, a sign of papal power which was increased in 1439 by news of the reunion of the Roman Catholic, Greek Orthodox, Mesopotamian and Chaldean Churches. The reunion proved shortlived and was never actually put into practice, but it helped to determine the crisis between Eugenius and the conciliarists, and the Council of Basle disintegrated. Fearing another schism, Felix left Basle in 1442 and seven years later he resigned even the pretence of his title.

The Council of Ferrara/Florence/Rome bowed completely to the papal will and it was dissolved sometime before the death of Eugenius in 1447 without naming a place or date for a future Council. It was to be almost exactly a century before the next Council met, at Trent. The bull *Execrabilis* of Pius II in January 1460 sealed the triumph of the Papacy.

There has sprung up in our time an execrable abuse, unheard of in earlier ages, namely that some men, imbued with the spirit of rebellion, presume to appeal to a future council from the Roman pontiff, the vicar of Jesus Christ, to whom in the person of blessed Peter it was said, 'Feed my sheep' and 'whatsoever thou shalt bind on earth shall be bound in heaven'. . . . We condemn appeals of this kind and denounce them as erroneous and destestable.

The conciliar movement was defeated, but it was not forgotten. Future popes were at great pains to ensure that no more Councils should be called and it was only in the critical years of the 1530s that Paul III agreed to summon another. The failure to convert the Church to constitutional rule not only re-established papal supremacy, but placed the means of reform more firmly than even in papal hands; it was the tragedy of the Church that, in this time of need, the Papacy was to be found wanting as never before.

The most obvious cause of the failure of the conciliar movements was the disunity of the conciliarists themselves, and their unwillingness to risk another schism; opposing each other on nationalistic lines, they disagreed on the details of reform, and thus the Papacy was able to overcome them. Moreover, by granting concordats to the various nations the Papacy deprived the movement of princely leadership, and it so happened that, at the time of the Bull Execrabilis, Pius II secured the friendship of the Emperor, Frederick III – which emphasised that reform and religious change was dependent upon the attitude of the ruling princes. Having achieved their personal aims, to some degree or another, few princes were sufficiently concerned to work for further reform. The Spanish monarchy of Ferdinand and Isabella was to be a notable exception but the rest, while not being entirely happy about papal supremacy, accepted the need for strong leadership and unity within the Church.

[6] THE FORCES OF REVIVAL

Since the established Church seemed to contradict the simplicity of the early Church of Christ there was, in the fifteenth century, a great revival of groups, practising poverty and seeking God in a direct and mystical way. Although these mystical groups lacked international organisation, their importance in the reform of the Catholic Church was very great. They had, in common with Wyclif and Huss, a contempt for the hierarchy, but rarely did they attempt to leave the Church, choosing instead to remain within it as a living example of what the Church ought to represent. Mysticism and a belief in poverty were by no means new but whereas early medieval groups tended to be drawn from the clergy themselves, the initiative in the fifteenth century, was taken by the laity, and unlike many of the earlier groups, like the Benedictine monks or the Franciscan friars who had become international, the new societies remained more localised.

The revival of mysticism may also have been partly produced by the Black Death and the falling population of the fourteenth and early fifteenth centuries which created a climate of spiritual depression and introspection. Be that as it may, corporate groups, usually of laymen, appeared all over Europe, but chiefly in the Rhineland and Netherlands, devoted to living strictly to Christ's pattern, as revealed in the Bible, and to helping others; a study of the scriptures was therefore important, as also was the use of the vernacular in teaching.

The Brethren of the Common Life, whose establishment in the Netherlands owed much to the work and ideals of Ruysbroeck (1293–1381) and Groote (1340–84), founded houses at Deventer, Delft, Zwolle and in many other places. The members of these communities took no vows, but voluntarily accepted the ideals of the society which laid little stress on the sacraments, on ceremony or on theological argument; instead, the Brethren lived quiet lives of piety and prayer, placing such great emphasis on book learning that they acquired a reputation all over western Europe for the standard of their education. In this, and in their stress upon the individuals' relationship with God they were humanistic, and they counted amongst their members such figures as Nicholas of Cusa (1400–64) and Erasmus (1466–1536). Moreover, the Brethren were essentially practical men who worked within the world.

Similarly, the group known as the Friends of God, whose greatest houses were at Cologne, Basle and Strasbourg and whose greatest figure was Tauler (1300–61), endeavoured to lead truly Christian lives and to set standards in their worship for others to follow. The third group of particular merit was the House of Canons Regular at Windesheim in the Netherlands, founded in 1386.

From this house sprang others, and from one of these came Thomas à Kempis (1379–1471), the most brilliant and famous mystic of the period. His work *The Imitation of Christ*, was the most complete expression of Netherlands fifteenth-century mysticism; it epitomised the atmosphere of quiet prayer, practical common sense, service to the community and holiness which was the essence of the various groups. Not that he was the only great writer of the place or period; the mystical writings of Meister Eckhart (1260–1327), a west German, of Suso (1300–66) and of Tauler (1300–61) all displayed the same attributes. Many of these writers had their origin in the fourteenth century, but, as symbolised in the work of Thomas à Kempis, the mystical groups of the Netherlands and Rhineland reached their peak in the fifteenth century. They were essentially revivalist movements directing their activities at those points where the organised Church failed, but they remained orthodox, and, although they may have disapproved of the Church's practices, they did not seriously question its doctrine, and many of the leaders found such favour with the establishment as to be canonised.

Elsewhere, mysticism tended to rest more on the individual, yet the aims and work were generally the same. Margery Kemp (d. 1440) was an illiterate Norfolk woman who claimed to have visions from God, which she dictated to a priest; Juliana of Norwich (d. 1413) wrote the *Revelation of Divine Love*, and likewise claimed direct inspiration from God; St Bridget of Sweden

(1303–73) and St Catherine of Siena (1347–80) were both mystics
who led attacks on abuses and who tried to establish godly
communities. All over Europe these groups and individuals
showed an example of holiness and religious fervour, but they
could only point the way and set the example. It was clear that
there was sufficient energy within the Catholic faith to revive it,
but only if pope or prince would provide the leadership.

In addition to the new societies, attempts were made to revive
and purify the older institutions of monks and friars. This happened particularly within the Franciscan Order where a group,
known as the Observants, who insisted that the order should
return to its original vows of poverty and godliness, revivified
the ideal of good works, charity and preaching and, after tremendous internal conflicts, gained control of the whole Order by
1517. Their greatest leaders were Bernardino of Siena (d. 1444),
who gained the reputation of being the finest preacher of his day
and Ximenes (1436–1517), the Archbishop of Toledo, who
reformed not only the Spanish Franciscans but the whole Spanish
Church. In the meantime, a separate group, the Minims, were
founded in 1474, vowed specifically to follow the poverty and
ideals of St Francis. Attempts at reform were not limited to the
orders themselves; Nicholas of Cusa, as a cardinal in 1448 and
legate for Germany in 1450, carried out extensive visitations,
and attempted to set standards of supervision for other bishops
and clergy to follow.

Another important attempt at revival, but not properly in
the main stream of European mysticism, was led by Savonarola
(d. 1498) in Florence. He was a Dominican friar who, in his
sermons, denounced the corruption of the clergy, the worldliness
of the Church and its lack of pastoral work. Despite the glories of
Renaissance Florence, much poverty and ignorance, made
worse from time to time by visitations of the plague, still existed,
and, in these circumstances, Savonarola found a following,
especially since his prophesies seemed to hold out some hope for
the poor and needy.

His opportunity came when the French invaded Italy and
expelled the Medici from Florence in 1494. Savonarola had

prophesied the end of the Medici and, thanks to the support of their enemies and of the French, he came to rule the city for four years. He proclaimed the kingdom of Jesus Christ and he set up a rigorously pure regime in which books were burned, plays banned and every attempt made to force the citizens to lead more puritanical lives.

Such a revival could not last. Opposition within the city grew and linked itself to Pope Alexander VI who was, in any case, preparing for action. Savonarola represented the underprivileged but they could do little to help him; flushed with power he became unbalanced and less in control of the situation, and so, in 1498, he was taken by some leading citizens, handed over to the papal commissioners and burned for heresy.

Although at times Renaissance Italy might seem to have been pagan, Savonarola's short lived movement, and the seventy-seven other fifteenth-century Italians, who were canonised for their good lives, illustrate that this was not so and they bear witness to the depth of religious feeling.

For all these societies and individuals, the sermon was the primary means of teaching the Christian faith – just as it had been to the friars in their heyday; nevertheless many of the reforming and revivalist groups placed much emphasis on a study of Christ's teaching as revealed in the Bible which was greatly stimulated by the work of men of the Renaissance, both south and north of the Alps. The core of the Renaissance ideal was the discovery and study of the classics and, since textual accuracy was all important, a tradition arose of examining the texts in a scientific and historical manner, and it was inevitable, in an age as religious as the fifteenth century, that these methods would soon be applied to the Bible.

Much dispute revolved around the interpretation of the Scriptures, and men were therefore led to query the accuracy of the various texts available and, where necessary, to return to a more accurate text. Although there is no direct demonstrable link between Renaissance and either Reformation or Counter Reformation, the knowledge and techniques acquired within the Renaissance assisted the creation of the atmosphere which shaped both movements. By the mid-fifteenth century, men such as Lorenzo Valla (1406–64) had already worked on biblical and allied texts, the greatest single discovery being the proof that the *Donation of Constantine* was a forgery, and as the fifteenth century continued on its course, more and more scholars turned to study the Bible in an historical manner, in order to establish textual accuracy. In this way the Bible and Christ's teaching were replaced at the centre of Christianity. By the early sixteenth century, helped by the advent of printing, the Bible was being regularly translated into all the European languages so that the literate population could read and interpret for themselves; thus the flood gates to individual study and interpretation were opened. This, a revival of religion in itself, represented a thrilling challenge to the Church which was compelled to re-assess its authoritarian attitude to the laity.

As the standard of lay education improved, so the laity became more unwilling to accept the Church as it then was. Between 1450 and 1517, nine new universities were founded in Germany and seven in Spain; in Sweden the university of Uppsala was founded, and many of the colleges of Oxford and Cambridge date from this period. Princes were educated by lay people and civil administrations fell into the hands of laymen like los Cobos in Spain and Thomas Cromwell in England. The Church thus became less able to dominate Europe intellectually, and the ignorance of the clergy became more obvious. The lawyers, especially, protested at clerical privileges such as immunity from the civil law, and the way in which laymen could be tried in church courts for 'moral' offences, while church taxes were more and more resented. By the early sixteenth century, such anti-clericalism had reached hitherto unknown proportions in western Europe.

The secular princes of Europe could well have taken the lead in reform had they so desired, but generally they did not. In England, Henry VI was pious but little interested in reform, and thereafter the Wars of the Roses distracted attention from such matters. Even after Henry VII's accession in 1485, there was usually more pressing business in hand and in any case,

Henry viewed the Church as an ally and did not wish to add the Papacy to the already considerable list of his enemies. Furthermore, he possessed sufficient control over the Church through his power to appoint its leaders who, in the persons of Fox, Warham and Morton, were among his most trusted advisers, and he was therefore unlikely to initiate reform, despite any pressures which might be brought on him. It was not until a political issue arose which brought a clash of interests between monarchy and Papacy in the reign of Henry VIII, that the Crown was at last prepared to consider violent reform or change. This is not to say that no reform went on in England, but without the active leadership of the Crown, it was inevitably piecemeal and incomplete.

In France the Valois monarchy was able to make agreements with the Papacy which proved politically satisfactory. The Pragmatic Sanction of Bourges in 1438 left the French Catholic Church almost independent of papal control, and although modified by the Concordat of Bologna in 1516 to allow more papal influence, particularly in its right of taxation, the power of high appointments remained with the monarch. Thus the royal government saw the Church as an ally and one, therefore, not seriously to be tampered with, despite the humanist leanings of Francis I or Margaret of Navarre.

In Austria and Germany a few half-hearted attempts at reform were made by princes. Frederick the Pious of Brunswick (1445–78) withdrew to a monastery founded by himself, but on a national scale he achieved little; Duke Albert of Austria (Emperor 1438–9) attempted a reform of certain monasteries but without much success, while Emperor Maximilian I (1493–1519), in trying to centralise his authority, showed willingness to accept a national German Church, but nothing came of it. Even his devout grandson, Charles V (1519–55) found it impossible to carry out a widespread reform; too much power rested with the individual German princes, and for the most part, they showed little interest in reform itself. Not until Luther offered them political power over their Churches did they evince a desire for change.

Similarly, in Italy there was no central body, except the Papacy, to initiate reform and the separate princes were too deeply involved in entrenching and increasing their own power, and too interested in the art and culture of the Renaissance. Savonarola's brief rule in Florence proved merely to be an important exception. Only in Spain did the monarchy show itself able and willing to carry out a far reaching reform.

After the union of the Crowns of Castile and Aragon in 1479, Ferdinand set about the task of reducing the country to royal control. This process of centralisation naturally included the Church, and, for over thirty years, Ferdinand played a diplomatic game with the Papacy, in which he gradually brought the immensely powerful and wealthy Spanish Church under royal control. Endowed with enormous tracts of land, the Church included seven archbishops and forty bishops, the Archbishop of Toledo, primate of the Spanish Church being second only to the King in power. Moreover, the leading clergy had proved themselves able military leaders in the long struggle against the Moors who, by 1479, were restricted to a small area of Granada in the south.

The Church in Spain was always wary of papal power, while the Papacy was unwilling to annoy Ferdinand because of its designs in Italy, for which it needed Ferdinand's support or neutrality. Ferdinand was thus able to play the Spanish Church and the Papacy off against each other, and this he did most skilfully. In 1478 an ecclesiastical council at Seville approved the royal plan to take control of all appointments and benefices in Castile. There followed a tremendous struggle between Crown and Papacy, in particular concerning the appointment of the Bishop of Cuenca, over which the pope gave way in 1482. Making insufficient headway, however, Ferdinand changed his mode of attack. All was nearly ready for the final conquest of Moorish Granada, and Ferdinand therefore claimed that, as a reward for its crusading zeal, the Crown should receive the right of appointment in Granada. This, the Papacy granted in 1486, and Ferdinand used it as a precedent to be extended elsewhere.

In 1493 Spain received the sole right to convert the recently discovered Indies; in 1501 the right to all tithes from them and seven years later Julius II granted full power of appointment to benefices in the New World. Thus the conversion and the Church of the New World were brought wholly under the control of the Spanish monarchy. Strengthened by these successes, Ferdinand usually managed to secure the acceptance of his nominees to bishoprics in Spain itself, and the final triumph came just after his death when, in 1523, Adrian VI granted to Charles V the official right of appointment of all bishops, although not to all benefices, and quarrels over these continued. By careful diplomacy, appeals to Rome were virtually ended. Probably most important of all, however, was the way in which the Crown managed to extract money from the Church, normally in the form either of the Cruzada tax or the Tercias Reales, the royal right to one third of all tithes collected in Castile. In addition, the clergy often paid the subsidio, a tax on clerical incomes.

Ferdinand further extended his power through the Inquisition. Established directly under royal control in Castile in 1478 it was specifically aimed against Jews, especially those who nominally accepted Christianity; after a bitter struggle with the provincial authorities Ferdinand succeeded in extending it to Aragon in 1487, when a permanent Inquisitor was placed at Barcelona. And so, when many of the princes elsewhere in Europe were endeavouring to control their own Churches, and often embraced Lutheranism in order to do so, the Spanish monarchy already had sufficient control and no further readjustments were necessary. This suggests that Ferdinand's motives were primarily political, but this must not obscure the fact that he was devout, or, more important, that his wife Isabella was passionately interested in reform; it was largely under her patronage that it was carried out.

It was inevitable that, in a country which, for centuries, had successfully waged a crusade against the Moors, a sense of holy mission should arise. Thus there was considerable zeal to give backing to Isabella's leadership. Pluralism, absenteeism, ignorance of the clergy and many other abuses were present and so, when Isabella's confessor, Hernando de Talavera, urged the

Queen to initiate reform, she committed herself to raise the moral and educational standards of the clergy. Since the Crown was able to influence the appointment of bishops, a natural first step was to attempt to appoint men who were of spiritual quality, and this Isabella tried to do, although not with complete success. In 1484 the College of Santa Cruz, which became the model for similar colleges elsewhere in Spain, was founded at Valladolid to train and educate the clergy.

In bringing reform to the great religious orders, the significant figure was Ximenes de Cisneros, who became Isabella's confessor in 1492. Ximenes, Archbishop of Toledo in 1495 and Cardinal in 1507, remained, until his death in 1517, the strong man within the Spanish Church, and, even after Isabella's death in 1504, he ensured that the work of reform continued. Although not a humanist in the true sense, Ximenes realised that the Church must move with the times and accept and use the new learning and higher standards of education. His first main work was within his own order – the Franciscans. As an Observant friar, Ximenes willingly accepted the papal and royal invitation to purify the order, with the result that between 1493 and 1506, he succeeded in imposing on the Franciscans strict observance of the rules of the order, and a return to the purity of the original foundation. Inevitably, this influence spread to other orders and the Dominicans and Benedictines benefited accordingly. By Ximenes's death in 1517 not only were the great orders reformed, but, proof of the zeal amongst the population, their numbers were rising.

In this early stage of reform Erasmus's ideas had great impact upon the orders and, in this way, much of the new learning of classical and Christian humanism penetrated Spain. This was increased by the foundation of the University of Alcala in 1508, specially for theologial studies, and the publication of the Complutensian Polyglot Bible in which the Greek, Hebrew and Latin texts were printed side by side. These reforms came at a vital stage for Spain, just when discontent with the Church elsewhere was growing to serious proportions. Thus when Luther, and later Calvin, burst on the scene they had little success in

Spain since the work of reform was accomplished and Spain therefore avoided the religious upheaval which other countries suffered. This was not without cost, however, for during the 1530s the Church became stiflingly orthodox, and a restrictive influence on Spanish society.

A less laudable side of the reform movement initiated by Isabella was the attack on the Jews. The religious fervour of the late fifteenth century helped to bring to the surface a long standing resentment against the Jews to such an extent that the Inquisition was established principally to deal with them. The culmination came in 1492, when an edict was issued expelling non-Christianised Jews entirely from Spain which thus became nominally wholly Christian, but the loss of the skill and industry of the Jews proved disastrous.

To Isabella, the conquests in America appeared in the form of a crusade, and she hoped to be able to attack the power of Islam from the direction of the New World, where the work of the missionaries provided a striking tribute to the energy of the Spanish Church. The early sixteenth century was the golden age of the friars in the Americas. Starting with a group of twelve only, the movement increased amazingly, some of the finest minds of the religious orders leaving Spain to convert the native populations. Zumarraga, a Franciscan, and later first Bishop of Mexico, was an Erasmian humanist who carried with him a vision of creating in Mexico the perfect Christian community; the Dominican, Antonia de Montesinos, pleaded as early as 1511 for the humane treatment of native Indians, and his cries were taken up by others, the most notable of whom was another Dominican, Bartholome de las Casas, who argued that the Indians should have the same rights as any other Spanish citizens. It was largely through the work of the Church that slavery was radically reduced, and that, by means of the New Laws for the Indies passed in 1542, the almost feudal land organisation of Spanish America, based on the encomienda system, was broken up.

By 1559 in Mexico alone, 800 Friars and almost 500 secular clergy were present, and it is estimated that 300 churches had

been built and nine million souls converted, although how deeply
is debatable; European and Christian belief had been assidu-
ously taught and the native population had been exposed to the
most liberal and humanist thought of sixteenth-century Europe.
In the long run, however, the growth of the Church was hampered by the failure to create enough priests from the Indians
themselves.

[7] REFORM FRUSTRATED,
THE FAILURE OF LEADERSHIP

Western Europe thus contained considerable piety and religious
energy, but little could be achieved without a lead from the
Papacy and the characters of the popes themselves therefore
became a vital factor. Martin V (1417–31) was responsible for
overcoming the conciliar movement and this, rather than reform,
was his main task. He was succeeded by the austere Eugenius
IV (1431–47) who continued the suppression of the conciliarists,
reached agreement with the Hussites and the Greek Orthodox
Church, but was faced with the loss of Rome itself. He was
driven out in 1434, and it was only after military conquest that
he managed to return in 1443. Thus, despite his interest in
reform of the Curia and of the religious orders, he had little
opportunity to initiate constructive work in these areas,
although he remained an important figure in the history of the
Papacy. His successor, Nicholas V (1447–55), was more interested in the art and letters of the Renaissance, and, having gained
his position through his reputation as a scholar, he founded the
Vatican library and raised the prestige of the Papacy, but he
thereby distracted it from its true duties.

Calixtus III (1455–58) began with great ideas for crusade, but
these soon cooled and he is chiefly remembered for his nepotism
towards his family, the Borgias. On the other hand, Pius II
(1458–64) is regarded by some as the last great pope of the
Middle Ages. He was responsible for the Bull Execrabilis and

for the final defeat of the conciliar movement and he showed
enthusiasm for a crusade; his humanist writings enlarged the
cultural reputation of the Papacy but, despite his undoubted
ability, he failed to produce the spiritual leadership which was
so badly needed, although when he died he was about to embark
on a crusade.

Paul II (1464–71) tried to purge the papal administration of
those who had entered it solely to advance their study of art and
letters but quarrels amongst the cardinals handicapped him and
ultimately Paul proved too interested in his own pleasures.
Thereafter, the Papacy became inextricably involved in the
growing disorder within Rome and, dazzled by the attractions
of the Renaissance, it entered a period of tragic moral decline.

Francesco Della Rovere, an observant Franciscan of humble
origins who rose in the Church through a reputation for piety,
learning and for his theological writings was elected pope as
Sixtus IV (1471–84), yet, once in office, his attitude seemed
to change completely. Appearing more as an Italian prince than
as pope, he became involved in family struggles, especially
against the Medici, and on increasing his own power. A
violent man, he practised nepotism and extortion on a hitherto
unprecedented scale and showed a minimal interest in the
spiritual affairs of the Church. His successor, Innocent VIII
(1484–92) carried corruption even further as Rome was dragged
down by the feuds of its leading families. The advancement of
his family proved to be Innocent's prime aim and, having
openly acknowledged his children, he found for his son a Medici
wife. Financial exaction reached its height. Indulgences and
pardons, even for murder, were sold to such an extent that the
papal vice-chamberlain is said to have remarked, 'The Lord
desireth not the death of a sinner, but rather that he may live
and pay'.

Alexander VI (1492–1503) was a gifted but misguided per-
sonality who, after recognising his children, devoted his efforts
to enlarging the fortunes of the Borgia family. His son, Caesar
Borgia, was renowned throughout Italy for his political ambitions and for his complete lack of scruple; incest, murder and

brutality were amongst the charges levelled at him, but he was unable to prevent the election in 1503 of della Rovere, his father's greatest rival. Although Julius II (1503–13) was less obviously corrupt than Innocent or Alexander he was at least as damaging to the papal reputation. Known as the 'warrior pope'; he did much to centralise papal authority in central Italy, and in 1507 he personally led the conquest of Bologna. A warlike, passionate man, possessing great energy and administrative ability, Julius became the centre of diplomatic intrigue and his system of alliances prolonged war in Europe; more than any other pope, he was entirely the Italian prince, and Europe was shocked by his behaviour. He fell into such disrepute that the conciliar movement once again raised its head.

In 1511 certain cardinals, backed by Louis XII of France, summoned a General Council to Pisa; Julius countered in 1512, by summoning a Council to meet in the Lateran at Rome. In this trial of strength he was successful. Louis XII's Council collapsed owing to the fact that only French supporters attended it, and Julius even considered deposing Louis and presenting the French throne to Henry VIII. Thus, while Julius dragged down the papal reputation, he proved the strength of the Papacy both politically and within the Church. Moreover, almost by accident, a Council had been called, although it remained to be seen how much reform it might achieve.

This fifth Lateran Council was opened by Julius in 1512, but since he died in the following year, its direction was left to Leo X (1513–21). Leo, a Medici, and the greatest of all papal patrons of the Renaissance, subjected all else to the pursuit of letters and the consequent glorification of the Papacy and of his family. Every source of income was exploited to provide for the magnificent rebuilding of St Peter's in Rome, and the sale of indulgences reached new heights. It became increasingly obvious that the chief aim of papal policy was the raising of money and it was on this very issue that Luther made his stand in 1517. On the other hand, Leo was pacific by nature, and the warlike activities of Julius were not continued. As for the Lateran Council, little was achieved.

Nevertheless, Catholics throughout Europe took the Council seriously. Giles of Viterbo, the General of the Augustinians, spoke forcefully in favour of reform while the Spanish delegation was instructed to press for a thorough reform of the Curia. A bull was issued in 1514 which contained many sensible measures concerning the extravagance of the cardinals, the evils of sorcery and superstition and the lack of education of the clergy:

With the approval of the holy council we decree and ordain that no clerics, whether seculars or members of any mendicant orders or any other order to which the office of preaching pertains by right, custom, privilege or otherwise, be admitted to exercise that office unless they have first been carefully examined by their respective superiors and found competent and fit as regards moral integrity, age, knowledge, uprightness, prudence and exemplariness of life. . . .

The unlicensed printing of books was attacked and various statements on morals made, but it was all on too limited a scale. Thus the Council gave opportunity for many to express their concern at the state of the Church, and it provided further evidence of the profound desire for reform on the eve of Luther's protest, but when the bishops and clergy began to quarrel, Leo dissolved it in 1517.

Thus in the crucial period, at the end of the fifteenth and the beginning of the sixteenth century, the Papacy lapsed into its greatest decline since the days of the Schism. It fell into the hands of rival and ambitious Roman families who, while often politically able and culturally sensitive, totally neglected the spiritual life of the Church and the urgent need for reform. In the years after 1517 the situation became critical as Luther's ideas split the Church and divided Europe; the need for effective leadership became essential to the very preservation of the Roman Catholic Church and of the Papacy itself.

Principal Events

1270–1342. Life of Marsilio of Padua
            1324. *Defensor Pacis* written
1300–49.   Life of William of Occam
1320–84.   Life of Wyclif
1369–1415. Life of Huss
1409.   Council of Pisa
1414–18.   Council of Constance
            1415. Decree *Sacrosancta*
1423–4.   Council of Pavia/Siena
1431–47.   Council of Basle/Ferrara/Florence/Rome
1439.   Reunion of Roman Catholic, Greek Orthodox, Chaldean
            and Mesopotamian Churches
1460.   Bull *Execrabilis*
1379–1471. Life of Thomas à Kempis
            Imitation of Christ written
1400–64.   Life of Nicholas of Cusa
1466–1536. Life of Erasmus
1494–8.   Savonarola's rule in Florence
1478.   Inquisition in Castile
1479.   Marriage of Ferdinand and Isabella, and Union of
            crowns of Castile and Aragon
1479–1504. Isabella, Queen of Spain
1436–1517. Life of Ximenes, Archbishop of Toledo
1512–17.   Fifth Lateran Council

PART III

Sixteenth-century Reform before Trent, the Movement Gathers Pace

[8] THE CHALLENGE OF LUTHER

Luther's views were as much a reaction to the state of the late medieval Church as were those of the most devout Catholic theologians; he produced ideas which, although not new, were acceptable to the age in which he lived, and if the Catholic Church hoped to retain its position it was essential that it should also do so.

Although no humanist, Luther's denial of the necessity of the Church as an intermediary between God and man, his almost mystical accent on man's own ability to find God and his translation of the Bible into German were at one with the ideas of the north European humanists of his time. His simple services carried on in German, his attacks on superstition, his bitter invective against the way in which the Papacy was draining Germany of money appealed to the educated laity, while justification by faith alone appeared to remove from man's shoulders the onerous responsibility for obtaining salvation. Luther's view of the relationship between Church and state – perhaps the most important aspect of all – gave more power to the prince than the Papacy had done with the European nations in the fifteenth century while even the spectre of conciliarism was raised again by Luther's denial of the papal supremacy, moreover it was largely this issue which had caused the summoning of the Lateran Council which was only dissolved in 1517, the very year of Luther's protest. As time passed many of his views appeared beyond the pale of orthodox Catholicism, but this was not necessarily apparent early on, and many leading Catholics felt that compromise was possible at least until the 1540s.

Nevertheless Luther touched the Church on too many sore spots, and it therefore moved too readily to its own defence. In 1518 Luther was allowed a public debate with Cardinal Cajetan at Augsburg, and in the following year the celebrated Leipzig debate with the famous theologian John Eck took place. By January 1521 the Papacy had presented its ultimatum to Luther and had publicly excommunicated him. Already the Church had failed to resolve its greatest problem, however; not only had it helped enlarge and advertise Luther's views but, worse still, it had neither compromised with them, drawing them into the orthodox framework of the Church, nor eradicated Luther himself. As the 1520s progressed, it became obvious that the latter course was impossible. Consequently the Papacy was faced with an ever worsening situation in which Luther's ideas, already deemed heretical, found more and more favour all over Europe to the great loss of prestige and, more importantly, of revenue. The need for reform and reinvigoration was more apparent than ever before; never was effective leadership by the Papacy so necessary.

The movement for reform was initiated not in any one part of Europe but in several, of which Spain and Italy were the most important, and this movement owed its origins not to Lutheranism or to any other form of Protestantism, but to the general dissatisfaction with the Church, of which Luther himself was a product. This does not eliminate, however, the idea that the Protestant Reformation profoundly affected both the speed and the direction which the Church's own reform took; indeed the need to combat the new Protestant Churches goes some way to explain the narrow and strictly orthodox character which the Counter Reformation ultimately assumed.

Protestantism so rent the Roman Catholic Church that it was essential that reform should come more quickly, and what happened after 1517 was a gradual quickening of reform impulses, growing to an absolute demand that the Papacy should act. Nevertheless Luther's protest did not immediately provoke the Papacy into reform, and the improvement in standards within the Church rested for a while yet on the piecemeal work of devoted individuals, and on the new or recently reformed orders and societies. Nowhere was this more true than in Italy itself, where, significantly, the leaders of the new orders were men who were later to achieve high ranking position within the hierarchy from which they could provide the much needed lead.

[9] THE NEW ORDERS

At the same time as Savonarola's revival in Florence (see page 42) devout Christians in other Italian cities were joining together in order to improve their own lives and to carry out works of charity. Such groups, more commonly known as oratories, formed themselves at Vicenza in 1494, and at Genoa in 1497 under the leadership of St Catherine of Genoa who taught that the soul should be consumed with a totally disinterested love of God, and that that love should be allowed to express itself in works of charity. Hospitals were founded in the city and the members of the oratory moved about amongst the poor and needy taking with them both spiritual and material comfort. The Genoan oratory proved to be the starting point for many others when St Catherine's disciple, Vernazzi, took the message to Rome where the most important of the oratories was formed in 1517.

Known as the Oratory of the Divine Love, it was initially a society for both clergy and laymen where worship, especially in the form of methodical prayer was carried on and charitable works planned. It quickly attracted people of great prominence, some even from the Papal Curia itself. Carafa, the Bishop of

Chieti, Sadoleto, later a model Bishop of Carpentras and at this time secretary to Leo X, Giberti, later secretary and chief adviser to Clement VII and Bishop of Verona, and di Thiene were all early members who began to set new standards of worship and good works to their contemporaries. As in Genoa, the members vowed themselves to an austere and pious life in which they would seek God through a personal struggle to purify themselves and an attempt to help others; soon a hospital for incurables was founded in Rome, and alms and poor relief were taken all over the city.

The members of the Roman and other oratories, while taking communal vows, did not live communally; they carried on their normal occupations at the same time as doing the work of the oratory. Nevertheless, the vows they took served to invigorate and purify their own lives. Furthermore, as members of such groups they had the confidence which arises from a corporate purpose, and as a group they were able to accomplish more than would have been possible individually.

Similar oratories soon appeared in other parts of Italy. In Venice a group formed under the layman diplomat, Contarini, who, although not a member of the Roman oratory, was connected with it. Contarini was later to be amongst the most prominent reformers of the Counter Reformation, and a figure of international reputation. In southern Italy the Community of Camaldoli arose, many of its instigators having been friends of Contarini, while in Naples a similar group appeared. In Rome itself, certain members of the Oratory of the Divine Love joined together in 1524 to form the Congregation of Clerks Regular, often known as the Theatines. Battista da Crema, the author of such devotional tracts as *Self Knowledge and Self Conquest* and *The Interior Mirror*, with Carafa and di Thiene, was amongst the founders of the Congregation who took their vows of poverty and chastity and determined to reform their own lives and the lives of others. Methodical prayer and worship and pastoral work were again the main themes of the group who, like the oratory, continued their normal occupations as well as carrying out religious vows; their influence was soon felt outside Italy and branches of the Congregation appeared in Spain, Portugal and Germany.

While these new orders were being formed, de Bascio led an important splinter group away from the old Franciscan Order. Known as the Capucins, this group, receiving its constitution in 1529 and formal recognition in 1536, worked amongst the poor and destitute, gaining a reputation for vigour which made it unpopular with older, more conservative groups, especially within its own Franciscan Order. In 1542 the Capucins faced their greatest trial when their leader, Bernard Ochino, turned Protestant, but they survived and continued to flourish.

Throughout this period the originators of the Roman oratory and of the Congregation of Clerks Regular exerted widespread influence, Carafa helping to form both the Sommaschi in northern Italy in 1532 and the Barnabites, centred on Milan in 1533. Although the Sommaschi began their existence specifically to care for orphans, their work soon extended to general works of charity. The Barnabites carried out all kinds of charity but were most renowned for their open air processions and festivals and for their great evangelical meetings in and around Milan. Their reputation chiefly rested on their willingness to use any and every method of taking the word of God to ordinary people, whether through straightforward preaching or through the emotional enthusiasm aroused by visual spectacles. Since women played a great part in re-invigorating the life of the Church it was inevitable that a society for women should be founded and so, in 1535, Angela Merici formed the Ursulines, which gave women the opportunity to take communal vows and to carry out works of charity as an ordered group.

Perhaps the most attractive of the early Italian reformers, however, was Philip Neri (1515–95). Moving to Rome in 1532, he endeavoured, over a period of twenty years, and largely by his own example, to reform the Papal Curia. A flexible, moderate person with a sense of humour, he believed that every man should be allowed to develop his own special talents, thus, in 1548, he formed a brotherhood in Rome for prayer and discussion and to help the poor. To this order, officially recognised in 1564 as the Congregation of the Oratory, scholars and eminent men flocked and soon other houses appeared, first in Italy, then in France. For the example of his life and the effectiveness of his work Neri was later canonised.

The Italian groups may have received indirect influence from Spain and the Rhineland, but there is little doubt that their main impetus came from within Italy itself. Several appeared before Luther's outburst in 1517, and the events of the German Protestant Reformation played little, if any, part in shaping their characters or beliefs; as time passed this became less so since the leaders, realising that their Church was threatened by the Protestant movement, were forced to shape their actions in this light.

The most famous, most effective, of the new orders, however, was largely Spanish in origin. Sharing most of the characteristics of their Italian counterparts, including their lack of concern with Luther's actions in Germany, the Jesuits were very much the personal foundation of the Spaniard, Ignatius Loyola, who, going through spiritual turmoil in much the same manner as, but quite independently of Luther, reached very different conclusions.

Loyola was born about 1491 in the Basque province of modern Spain. As a soldier in the army of Navarre he was wounded in 1521, and it was while recovering from his injury – in fact his leg was never completely mended and straightened – that he read and studied works of religion which so interested him that in the years 1521 and 1522 he paid prolonged visits to the monasteries of Montserrat and Manresa in north-east Spain, and it was there that, while continuing his studies, he took his own personal vows and began to write what later became the handbook of the Jesuit Society, the Spiritual Exercises.

There has been much discussion concerning the influences upon Loyola during this and later formative periods. As the son of a modest landowning family he was undoubtedly exposed to traditional Spanish Roman Catholicism, and it is known that at Manresa he read works emanating from the Rhineland mystical and charitable groups, including Thomas à Kempis's

Imitation of Christ. Later, when he moved through the Middle East, parts of Spain, France and eventually Italy, his experience broadened so that, as is evident in his writings, he came to understand the problems, temptations and possibilities of the contemporary world. Few men so successfully adapted their aims and ideas to the life of sixteenth-century Europe; in doing so he created an organisation capable of meeting the Calvinists on equal terms.

Striving at Montserrat and Manresa in 1521 and 1522 with the problem of how best to reach God and serve the Church, Loyola chose an opposite path to Luther. Seeing the unity of the Church as all important he wrote in the *Spiritual Exercises*: 'Laying aside all private judgement, we ought to hold our minds prepared and prompt to obey in all things the true spouse of Christ our Lord, which is our Holy Mother, the hierarchical Church', and in another part of the same work: 'We ought always to be ready to believe that what seems to us white is black, if the hierarchical Church so defines it'. Out of this spiritual struggle Loyola's beliefs were forged, and he pledged himself to serve God and the Church in every way.

The way he chose was totally uninfluenced by any consideration of the Protestant Reformation in Germany; on the contrary, he determined to visit the Holy Land, hence part of 1522 was spent in Palestine. Deciding, however, to improve his education, he withdrew to the universities of Alcala and Salamanca where his views were questioned by the Inquisition, but, despite certain doubts and restrictions, he was in the event declared orthodox, and in 1528 was permitted to leave Spain to continue his studies at the university of Paris. There, he was the contemporary of John Calvin, although there is no evidence of them having met; still Protestantism seems to have played little part in the shaping of his aims.

In Paris, he became the leader of a small but devoted and extremely pious group of men who worshipped together, discussing the very essence of their religion. To these men Loyola's experiences and writings proved an inspiration, and so in 1534 ten of them, including Loyola, took common vows to serve the

Church and the Papacy, hoping more especially, to carry again the Christian religion to the Middle East. The other nine comprised the two Savoyards Favre and le Jay, two Frenchmen Brouet and Codure, the Portuguese Rodriguez, and four Spaniards Xavier, Lainez, Salmeron and Bobadilla. In the hope of obtaining papal blessing for their endeavour – together with a passage to Palestine – they travelled to Rome where, while awaiting the papal decision, they earned a considerable reputation by their work in the city's slums and by the standard of their learning

There were those at Rome who, fearing the vigour and possible independence of this new order, brought pressure to bear on Paul III to withhold recognition, but the liberal Contarini, by now a cardinal, together with Paul's own inclination triumphed, and in 1540 the Society of Jesus received its official charter. Lack of transport determined that the society should not go to the Holy Land; it was therefore dedicated to serving the pope when and where he should decree.

It was thus, almost by accident and certainly not by the design of its founder, that the Jesuits were employed to combat the Protestant Reformation. Nevertheless they never lost their crusading zeal. Although Brouet and Salmeron were sent to Siena, Faber and Lainez to Parma, Xavier and Bobadilla to the Campagna, while Loyola stayed in Rome, they soon found their way, not only to the rest of Europe, but to the New Worlds as well, indeed as early as 1542 Francis Xavier left to labour for the remainder of his life in the Far East.

At first, the society was limited to sixty, but this was relaxed in 1544 so that, by the 1550s, it numbered over one thousand. Such rapid growth is testimony both to the attraction of Loyola's teachings and to the depth of religious belief in mid-sixteenth-century Europe, for the way into the Jesuit Society was hard and its training long and testing.

The training was based upon the Spiritual Exercises, personally administered to every novice by an experienced Jesuit who, using them as a guide and a handbook, led the novice through the same experiences of spiritual striving which Loyola himself had undergone. In this way each novice was guided at the speed most suited to his ability and faith, which could last anything from six to ten years, or even longer.

The process started with two years of initial probation, during which period the novice was confronted with the *Spiritual Exercises*, and with the Bible itself from which the Gospels were examined in great detail. Within these two years, the most important points were the four stages when he was taken through the same actual experiences as Loyola; in the first stage – a week, or longer if the Jesuit considered it necessary – the novice was required to examine himself continually, to struggle against his worst self, to purge himself of his faults and to make a definite choice of God rather than of sin. In the second stage the kingdom of God and the standards required of man by God were deeply considered and accepted by the novice, and in the third stage further meditation was carried out to strengthen the resolve. The final stage was aimed to bring everything together, and the novice was to meditate on all aspects of God, His glory, His love and the Christian religion. During these four stages the entrant to the society was left to struggle within himself in order to make these fundamental decisions, but he was not left alone; always present was the Jesuit, armed with the *Spiritual Exercises* to help and to guide. The *Exercises*, indeed, contained not merely advice to be given to the novice, but advice also to the Jesuit on how best to help the novice.

Having completed the first two probationary years, the young Jesuit was then to study at a university to obtain a degree in some subject such as philosophy, followed by several years of theology at university leading to ordination. All this might occupy eight or nine years, but the Jesuit still had his final year of probation to serve before complete acceptance into the society. Having completed that year, he was at last allowed to make his vows. Not everyone took exactly the same vows, however. Some took the 'simple' vows, others, known as 'the professed' took additional vows, and it was these latter who elected the General Congregation, the senior members of the society who, in turn, elected the General or head of the society for life. Complete entry into the Society of Jesus was therefore unusually difficult, a man being required to surrender his possessions, his family, his passions and, if necessary, his life in the service of God and the Church.

It might be thought that in demanding strict obedience to the Papacy, Loyola would produce a society working blindly and unintelligently, but nothing was further from the truth, for Loyola believed in man's free will, in his ability to reach God through his own efforts; consequently Jesuits were trained to help men find God in their own way. This demanded, not only a highly educated mind but, above all, an extremely flexible approach. The Jesuits believed that God could be found anywhere, at any time, thus they were prepared to use all the senses and all means to bring the individual nearer to Him, which demanded that Jesuits should adapt themselves to whatever country or society they were in, and to whatever individual with whom they were dealing; hence strict obedience to the Papacy did not militate against the free agency of the Jesuit in the details of his work. Within the society itself the General, Loyola at first, then, on his death in 1556, Lainez, was in complete command, although it had not been Loyola's original intention that it should assume this military appearance. This situation only arose as the society's growth in size entailed the need for greater organisation.

By the early 1540s, the Jesuits had acquired a reputation, not only for their pastoral work and their own extensive education, but also for the education which they were able to provide for others. Loyola considered, like the Christian humanists of his time, that a full classical and liberal education was the best training for the understanding of the Christian faith, stressing also the importance of physical education to ensure that the body, as well as the mind, was prepared to carry out whatever was demanded of it. Thus the Jesuit education took full account of the new learning and new methods, especially of printing, and the colleges set up at Rome (1540), Vienna (1545), Cologne (1555) and Ingolstadt (1556) soon became famous for the standard of the education which they gave.

The new orders contributed greatly to the character of the whole Counter Reformation, yet there was much about them that was novel which distinguished them even from the reformed elements of the older orders of monks and friars. Loyola was both mystic and man of action; as such he typified the leaders of the early period of the Counter Reformation. Members of the oratories and other groups were deeply concerned with their personal relationships with God, and these they attempted to work out by the most stringent daily, personal routine of prayer, meditation and self examination. These routines involved an immense struggle with oneself where, assisted by God's grace, one attempted to overcome one's worst instincts and to bend one's will to God's. This personal, mystical worship – as much a reaction to the excessive pomp and ceremony of the late medieval Church as the mysticism of the Rhineland groups (see page 40) – which brought one close to God, was in harmony with the sixteenth century belief in individualism, but it by no means replaced the older corporate worship; indeed, even greater attention than before was paid to the confession and the mass.

The confessional was yet another means of baring oneself before God and of accepting that His will alone be done, while total involvement in the mass emphasised the supreme sacrifice which Christ had made for man. Members of the new orders placed such importance on the mass, as leading to a greater understanding of God, that they attended it daily, encouraging others to do so as often as possible.

The new orders also learned that to serve God properly and, from the 1540s on, to meet Protestantism effectively, it was necessary to place action before controversy, to make deeds speak louder than words, to do charitable works rather than to preach reform; in this way God could be glorified to the utmost. Consequently they established almshouses, schools and hospitals, and preached to the poor and needy wherever necessary. The Jesuit charter of 1540 specifically stated that, while each Jesuit must attend to the routine of daily prayers and services, the members did not need to be all in one place, thus they could roam the world, strengthened by the society as a whole, but not physically within it. The same was true of the other orders who, although taking communal vows, never lived in common; thus the new orders lived and worked within the world, whereas the majority of the medieval orders were withdrawn from it. Furthermore, the new orders, even the Jesuits, abandoned the uniform dress so that they would fit more easily into whatever society they found themselves, all of which enabled these orders to obtain a closer understanding of the world in which they lived, to use it where it would benefit true religion and to combat it where it would not.

Some of the older orders made positive attempts to reform and to re-invigorate themselves, often with considerable success. The Observant branch of the Franciscans, already mentioned in connection with Ximenes and reform in Spain (see page 48), continued to be active. Likewise the Carthusians, especially at their charterhouses in London and Cologne, did much to maintain standards of piety and devotion, yet neither they nor the re-formed Franciscans were able to make a real impact on the sixteenth century.

Reform in Italy was further stimulated by the work of individuals, several of whom were members of the recently formed societies. Foremost amongst these were a number of bishops, from whom Giberti and Sadoleto may be taken as examples. Giberti, as Bishop of Verona from 1524 to 1543 followed the normal procedure of residing in Rome, until the Sack of Rome in 1527 after which he returned to Verona, where he created a model bishopric. It was a novelty in itself for a bishop to reside in his diocese, but Giberti went further; by preaching regularly, by printing regulations for parish priests to follow and by extensive visitations he insisted that the clergy should improve their standards. Sadoleto, on the other hand, having withdrawn to his diocese of Carpentras, just outside Italy in 1527, to lead a life of study and contemplation, exerted a widespread influence and, although lacking the vigour of Giberti, he succeeded in bringing reform to the diocese.

Outside Italy there existed many other groups and individuals
pressing for reform of the Roman Catholic Church, often on
much the same lines as the Italian societies. Amongst these were
the Christian humanists of northern Europe, of whom the best
known was undoubtedly Desiderius Erasmus (1466–1536), a
Netherlander, born in Rotterdam and educated by the Brethren
of the Common Life. Moving around the countries of western
Europe, but settling at Basle in Switzerland, he was acknowledged as the foremost scholar of his day and, in particular, as a
classical and Biblical editor.

Having seen the corruption of the Church in the Netherlands
and in France and having suffered under the sterile and stifling
atmosphere of the theological faculty of Paris university in the
1490s, he began to attack the practices of the Church, demanding
that a General Council be summoned to initiate reform; moreover,
as a friend of the greatest scholars and princes of the day
Erasmus was well able to make his views known. *Enchiridion
Militis Christiani*, written in 1504, which described how the
Christian should order his life, was, in Erasmus's own words,
designed 'to show the way which leadeth straight into Christ'. It
taught that life was a war of the spirit wherein man's chief
weapons were prayer and knowledge which was to be acquired
not only from the Scriptures but from a study of the classics;
thus Erasmus brought about the important fusion between
Christian and newly discovered classical thought.

In *In Praise of Folly*, a brilliant satire on the practices of the
Church, published in 1511, and in many other works, Erasmus
stressed what he considered were the main elements in Christian
worship. He brushed aside the importance of ceremony, he
attacked the superstitious reliance on images and relics, he
denounced absenteeism and the worldliness and ignorance of the
clergy, and he taught that man's first duty was to understand
and obey Christ's teaching as revealed in Scripture.

Some have said that Erasmus saw Christ too much as a moral teacher, but this is unjust. It is true that he placed less accent on the sacramental and ceremonial side of the Church, and that he rarely examined its doctrine deeply, but he was essentially trying to help the common man find God; this he believed could best be achieved by stripping religion down to its fundamentals, namely to adherence to Christ's teaching. In 1516, he wrote:

I do not at all share the opinion of those who do not want laymen to read the Sacred Scriptures in the vernacular, as though Christ had taught something enigmatic to be scarcely understood by a few theologians. They seem to think that the Christian religion is best protected by ignorance. I wish all women would read the Gospels and the letters of Paul. I wish they would be translated into all the languages. I wish the peasant would sing them behind the plough, the weaver at his loom, the pilgrim on his way.

To Erasmus, therefore, the Scriptures were all important; thus in 1516 he published a critical edition of the Greek New Testament and a similar work on the letters of St Jerome, in order to help European scholars in their understanding of the Bible.

Erasmus's Roman Catholicism was of a liberal brand, taken up by reformers in many parts of Europe, but so liberal was it that to many, including Luther at first, it seemed to be within the definition of Protestantism. This was a mistaken view. Erasmus hoped to hold a conciliatory position between extremes, so that Luther's unconcern at splitting the universal Church appalled him. A close friend of More and Fisher in England, Erasmus grew depressed by the growing violence and extremism of the 1520s and 1530s, and the execution of his English friends by Henry VIII was a severe blow.

Unfortunately, although Erasmus's ability, his tolerance and his humanity are worthy of respect, he achieved little of practical value in reforming the Church; he advertised the faults within the Church, he helped, indeed, to point the way to purer and deeper religion, but he was too much alone. English scholars and Italians such as Contarini may have been close to his spirit of compromise and conciliation but, as even Contarini was to find, the 1530s and 1540s were not an age when tolerance was acceptable and within a decade of his death, Erasmus's works were banned in Spain and by the newly founded Roman Inquisition.

Erasmus had acquired many of his ideas from English friends, from More and Fisher, but especially from John Colet, the Dean of St Paul's. Colet agreed upon the need for a purer religion based more closely on the study of the Scriptures, stressing also, what the whole of Europe had come to realise, that the standards of the clergy must be raised. To this end he founded St Paul's School in London, and in his aims he found considerable support. Fisher, in addition to helping in the establishment of chairs of Divinity at both Oxford and Cambridge, was largely responsible for the foundation of St John's College, Cambridge. At the same time Fox helped to establish Corpus Christi College, Oxford. Meanwhile, as Bishop of Rochester, Fisher did what he could, but the see was too small and poor for much to be achieved and although both he and More were fine examples of Christianity in their lives and in their writings, neither possessed sufficient influence to bring about reform in England.

The dominant influences at this time were Wolsey and the King himself. Wolsey, personifying many of the evils of the sixteenth-century Church, had little interest in reform, while the King, although prepared to oppose Luther with the *Assertion of the Seven Sacraments* in 1521, being rewarded with the title 'Defender of the Faith' by a grateful Leo X, did so merely as an academic exercise. If anything, the situation deteriorated under Cromwell in the 1530s, when neither minister nor King were concerned with improving the condition of the Church, but only with the transference of its power and the deprivation of its wealth. Little, therefore was done by the time of the Council of Trent, and with control of the Church having passed directly to the monarchy, the prospects for future reform seemed bleak indeed.

Similarly, little was done in France. From the 1516 Concordat of Bologna, much of the control of the Church rested with the monarchy, and Francis I (1515–47) was chiefly concerned with foreign affairs, being careful to nurture his Protestant friends in Germany, although occasionally, as in the 1530s when the Protestants seemed to attack his royal authority, a burst of persecution occurred. Nevertheless certain individuals did attempt to get something done. Jean Standouck, a Netherlander educated by the Brethren of the Common Life, established communities of devout men and women in Paris, Valenciennes, Malines and Louvain to help encourage and improve the education of the French clergy, while Josse van Clichtove (d. 1543), a disciple of the Christian humanism of Erasmus, was Luther's chief opponent in France.

The work of reform in Spain (see page 46) had largely been done before Charles V's arrival in 1517, but under his rule the Spanish Church remained pure, if increasingly repressive. In Germany, however, progress towards reform came slowly, despite the wishes of Charles himself. During the 1520s and 1530s Lutheranism made great progress both as a political and as a religious movement; moreover, in his attempts to stem it and to reform the Church Charles was hampered not only by his commitments elsewhere and by the hostility of the French and the Turks, but also by the fact that no German prince was prepared to assist him for fear of increasing imperial power. None of the more important princes in Germany therefore were willing to champion the Catholic cause. Nevertheless, as elsewhere, there were individuals who saw the need for action.

John Eck, Professor of Theology at Ingolstadt university from 1510 to 1543, was a determined opponent of Luther; he had many humanist connections and it was thanks to him that a Bible was produced in German in 1537 designed for the use of Roman Catholics. John Cochlaeus (1478–1552) attacked Luther vigorously, but the most distinguished Roman Catholic German scholar of the period was John Reuchlin (1455–1522). Like Colet in England, he believed that a detailed study of the Scriptures would bring men to a true understanding of Christianity and so he studied not only Latin and Greek but also Hebrew, so that a more accurate interpretation of the Scriptures could be made. The appeal of these men was, however, limited and none was able to influence events decisively. Much of the responsibility therefore devolved on to the shoulders of the Emperor, Charles V.

As a devout Roman Catholic, Charles abhorred Luther and desired, probably above all else, to see the Church purified first in his own empire, then in all Christendom so that, ultimately reunited, it might mount a concerted attack on the Moslem Turk. His commitments, however, were too great and he was unable to rely on other leading Catholic powers; France was hostile while the Papacy, regarding him as a political threat in Italy, proved uncooperative for long periods of time. Charles, realising that he was powerless to reform the Church in Germany over the heads of the individual princes, therefore laboured for a General Council to be called, if possible to meet in Germany.

He never, however, fully understood the character of Lutheranism or the depth of its roots. Believing that reform would automatically bring the Lutherans back to the fold he compromised with them, especially at the diets during the 1520s, until such time as the Council should meet – a policy also dictated by his need for their support against the Turks. At the Diet of Augsburg in 1530 Charles even took part in the actual discussions, but to no avail.

Charles, therefore, hoped that the decisions of a General Council would reconcile the Lutherans, heal the rift in the Church and solve many of his German problems. Fearing such a successful outcome, France opposed the scheme whereas the Papacy disliked the idea because the Council might become too strong or Charles might dominate it; moreover, by the 1530s, the Lutherans opposed it because they had little further to gain. Nor were the difficulties overcome after 1534 when Paul III agreed to summon the Council, since it could not meet until Charles and Francis were at peace, a situation not reached until the Treaty of Crèpy in 1544.

In 1544, however, Charles was not in a position to persuade the Lutherans to attend and, in any case, the pope seemed likely to allow doctrine to be discussed as soon as the Council sat, a policy which Charles opposed since a definition of orthodox doctrine might finally alienate the Lutherans. Insisting that only matters of discipline be discussed to begin with, he quarrelled with the Papacy, and when the Council eventually met at

Trent he refused even to recognise its decisions. Thus, by the time of the Council's first meeting, Charles had in no way managed to advance reform of his Church. On the contrary, he stood at loggerheads with the Papacy; Lutheranism seemed firmly rooted in Germany and the Council was about to meet outside German soil and with no Lutherans in attendance.

In eastern Europe the Church found an active princely defender in the person of Sigismund I of Poland. Aided by John Laski (d. 1531), the Primate of the Polish Church and by Peter Tomicki (d. 1535), the Bishop of Cracow, stout resistance, buttressed by anti-German nationalism, was offered to Lutheranism. Furthermore, since King and bishops realised that firmer leadership and a better example were needed, requests were sent to Rome that the Pope should summon a General Council for the purpose of church reform.

While most European countries possessed groups who desired a reinvigoration of the Roman Catholic Church, only in Spain and Italy was the work at all advanced during the first three decades of the sixteenth century. In reality the situation was even more critical. England, although remaining within the Catholic faith had rejected the Roman Church, while the whole of Scandinavia, large areas of Germany and smaller areas of the Netherlands, France and eastern Europe had embraced Lutheran ideas. In such a crisis only the Papacy could provide the necessary leadership and throughout the 1520s men watched and prayed, but in vain.

[11]   THE PAPACY, THE REVIVAL OF LEADERSHIP

Adrian VI (1522–3), the last non-Italian Pope, reigned for too short a time to accomplish anything of lasting significance. His successor, Clement VII (1523–34), a Medici, floundered out of his depth into the sea of European politics, attempting to play off the powers against one another, but ending up under the

control of Charles V after the battle of Landriano in 1529 and
the Treaty of Cambrai in the same year. Although the Sack of
Rome in 1527 aroused the feeling that this was God's punishment
on the Church and upon the Eternal City, reform was still not
forthcoming as Clement, showing little awareness of what was
really needed, fought a delaying action against Charles over
summoning a General Council. Nor did there seem much hope
of improvement when Clement died in 1534.

Paul III (1534–49) was born Alexander Farnese in 1468.
Brought up in the cultural atmosphere of the Medici family in
Florence, his early career – he was a bishop at the age of twenty,
a cardinal and Treasurer General of the Church at twenty-five –
served to illustrate the corruption amongst the higher ranks of
the Church. A cultured and intelligent person, his interests
were typical of the Medici family and Michelangelo built the
Farnese palace in Rome for him. He was not ordained and he
seemed primarily interested in the advancement of his own
family. By 1520, however, changes had appeared. He accepted
Holy Orders, he said his first mass, he visited his bishopric of
Parma and he acquired the reputation of being a strong-willed
administrator and diplomat, so that he was almost elected pope
in 1523. Thus, on Clement's death, his election was virtually a
formality.

Despite his latterday interest in the Church and its affairs,
Paul's main interest still appeared to be in his own family and
in the culture of Rome, thus few saw in him the man who was to
rally the Church, to heed the wishes of the new orders and to
provide the leadership which would bring the long night of the
medieval Church to an end. It came as no surprise, therefore,
when, on his election, he made two of his fifteen year old grand-
sons cardinals. What came as more of a shock was his elevation
to similar positions at the same time of Fisher, Contarini,
Sadoleto, Carafa, Pole, Morone, Cervini and du Bellay, the
Bishop of Paris – all men who had for long preached reform.
These cardinals, several of whom had given life and character to
the new religious orders of Italy were now in a position to do the
same for the whole Church. Paul III had thus taken a first vital

step to reform. Furthermore, despite the opposition of many cardinals, in 1536 he summoned a General Council although it was nine years before it eventually met.

In carrying out these policies Paul's motives were not those of a disinterested reformer; he was well aware of the European crisis which faced his Church, its authority and its wealth, and it was this at least as much as his reforming instincts which led him to take action. To this extent reform came in response to the Protestant movement. Nevertheless, the men elevated to meet the challenge developed their beliefs before 1517, so from the pontificate of Paul, the Counter Reformation movement was both a reaction to Protestantism and a response to the demands of Catholic reformers uninfluenced by Luther's movement.

Paul continued his positive leadership by fostering the Barnabites and Ursulines in Italy, by protecting the Roman Oratory, which some had come to see as so liberal as to be heretical and, most important of all, by granting a charter to the Jesuits in 1540, despite opposition from within the Curia. His recognition and use of the Jesuits was one of his greatest contributions to the Counter Reformation, for without his support Loyola could never have been given such wide opportunities; moreover, by patronising these orders, by promoting devout and able men and by giving the necessary leadership, he created the atmosphere in which they could flourish.

Another of Paul's measures was to appoint, in 1537, a commission, the *Consilium de Emendenda Ecclesia*, to enquire into the faults of the Church and to suggest what remedies might be applied. Reformers, led by Contarini, dominated the commission, whose findings, published in 1538, dealt so honestly with the Church's failings that the Lutherans published them as propaganda. These findings were a landmark, in that high ranking members of the Church openly criticised the system upon which their own positions rested. The conclusions recognised clearly that until the standard of the clergy at all levels was improved, effective reform could not take place; thus it was recommended that the Papacy should divest itself of the dispensing power by which the right to ignore rules and regulations could be granted. Furthermore the Commission criticised the popes themselves, stating that 'It is not lawful for the Pope, the vicar of Christ, to make any profit out of the use of the keys granted to him by Christ', a condemnation of every pope in living memory. Paul himself was certainly not free from such a charge, for at that very time he was in the process of transferring the Duchy of Parma to his own family. In attacking the cardinals for pluralism, greed and inattention to duty, the members of the Commission were criticising their immediate associates and indirectly pointing the finger at the Papacy for permitting such a state of affairs. They asked 'And, Holy Father, how can you expect to be obeyed, and for abuses to be corrected when abuses are tolerated in these principal members of the Church?' They insisted that bishops should be resident in their dioceses, that they should ensure that parish priests carried out their pastoral functions, and they even stated that anyone about to take up a benefice should be properly qualified.

Monasteries were severely criticised for their inattention to correct routine, the evils inherent in the sale of indulgences and the dangers in the superstitious attachment to images were dealt with but, in accordance with their earlier views on charity, Contarini and the other members of the Commission stressed that the clergy must, above all, preserve the interests of their ordinary parishioners.

The findings of the Commission produced few immediate results. Paul officially accepted them and, in 1540, sent bishops living as absentees in Rome back to their dioceses, but otherwise he did nothing, probably because he was inclined to leave the work of reform to the General Council which he had already summoned. By this time too, Paul found distrust and disagreement amongst the cardinals as to the best course for future action. On the one hand Contarini, representing the liberal, Erasmian tradition was prepared to meet the Lutherans and even to make concessions to bring them back into the Church; on many points, indeed, he had considerable sympathy with them, especially in their Augustinian view of Justification by

Faith, for which some of his opponents were prepared to accuse him of heresy. Contarini, therefore, looked forward to the General Council when the Protestants would be present and when such discussions could take place.

Carafa, on the other hand, was the prime representative of the conservative section who, seeing no point in negotiating with the Lutherans, sought a vigorous purification of the Church, not by the Council, which Carafa thought was unnecessary and dangerous, but by the Papacy itself through a strict enforcement of the canon law. Once that was achieved, then the fight could be waged to bring the Protestants back into the Church. For the moment Contarini held the advantage, but not for long; the days of conciliation and compromise were almost over.

It was the practice in Germany to hold gatherings of leading Catholic and Protestant theologians in the hope of some compromise being achieved. At one of these, meeting in Regensburg (Ratisbon) in 1541, at the same time as the imperial diet, Contarini made his last, unavailing effort to reach a settlement. Melanchthon attended, supposedly to represent Luther, although he was far more prepared to compromise than his master, Bucer represented the Protestantism of the south German cities, and John Calvin attended as a friend of Bucer; the Catholic side was led by two liberal members of the Cologne school of theologians, Johannes Gropper and Julius von Pflug, the Bishop of Naumburg, together with Contarini himself. On certain issues such as papal supremacy, there would be immediate disagreement, so Contarini deliberately shelved such matters, concentrating instead on those issues where he thought a compromise might be arranged.

The most obvious was the question of justification where both Contarini and Gropper took a view which went some way towards the doctrine of Justification by Faith put forward by Luther, indeed Gropper had already produced a compromise known commonly as Double Justification. This attempted to combine the orthodox Catholic view that a justified man becomes righteous in himself with the Lutheran idea that no man can be completely justified until he has received the gift of God's own righteousness. The question of the usefulness of good works in acquiring justification was barely touched upon, but when both sides at Regensburg accepted Gropper's formula, it seemed like a triumph for Contarini's liberalism.

This was not to be, however, for neither Luther on the one hand nor the Papacy on the other was prepared to accept Double Justification, roundly condemning it and warning their respective delegates not to exceed their very limited commissions. Even Francis I bitterly protested, not from strict doctrinal beliefs, but from fear that such a solution might be the first stage in uniting Germany behind Charles V. In fact they had no cause to worry. The agreement on Double Justification was soon followed by disagreements on equally important matters, principally over the question of real presence in the mass where Contarini held firmly to the orthodox Catholic belief in trans-substantiation. The meeting thence broke up without consider-ing the most contentious issue, the position of the Papacy.

The failure of the Colloquy of Regensburg marks the failure of the liberals to dominate and direct the work of the Counter Reformation; within a year Contarini was dead (1542) and the aggressive spirit of Carafa took the lead. It was his conservative, repressive policies which dominated the way in which the Counter Reformation developed.

Carafa had viewed the proceedings at Regensburg with dis-may, and his belief that compromise only benefited the opposi-tion seemed strengthened with the conversion to Protestantism in 1542 of Ochino, the leader of the Capucin Order. He was thus able to persuade Paul to establish the Roman Inquisition in 1542. Modelled on the Spanish Inquisition, he and five other cardinals were given the title of Inquisitors General and em-powered to deal with any person suspected of heresy or of the slightest unorthodoxy by interrogation, imprisonment on suspicion, confiscation of property and, if necessary, even by execution. The Inquisitors were granted authority over clergy, religious orders and laymen of any social standing; trials were held in secret, both witnesses and accused being liable to torture; moreover the accused was presumed guilty until able to prove his innocence. As chief Inquisitor Carafa was authorised to appoint deputies wherever necessary, while he himself set an example of ruthlessness, decreeing that 'no man is to lower himself by showing toleration towards any sort of heretic, least of all a Calvinist', and proclaiming that 'even if my own father were a heretic I would gather the wood to burn him'. An Index of prohibited books was compiled which included not merely the heretical works of Protestant leaders, but significantly the liberal works of Erasmus, Rabelais, Henry VIII and Machiavelli.

Outside Italy the Inquisition had little effect but within the Italian states its impact was immediate and disastrous. Despite considerable opposition heresy hunts took place throughout the country, books were burned in enormous quantities, 10,000 on one Sunday morning at Venice it was boasted, and much that was liberal and creative in Italian society perished. Such action continued at an even greater pace during Carafa's pontificate between 1555 and 1559, when a reign of terror was instigated in which no priest of whatever rank could feel secure from papal wrath, so much so that Cardinal Seripando observed that the Roman Inquisition 'acquired such a reputation that from no other judgement seat on earth were more horrible and fearful sentences to be expected.'

It was highly significant for the development of Roman Catholicism that conservative policies dominated the Curia when the General Council was at last able to meet. Although Paul III had summoned the Council to Mantua in 1536 it had not yet assembled; Charles V and the Germans had argued that it should meet in Germany whereas papal supporters were determined that it should sit in Italy; Francis I, on the other hand, was still deeply suspicious of any Council lest it should in some way decrease the problems of his arch-rival Charles V. Furthermore no effective Council was possible until Francis and Charles were at peace.

In 1537 Paul met Charles and Francis at Nice, but no useful agreements were made, and between 1542 and 1544 the two great powers were again at war. Despite this Paul saw that, such was the crisis confronting the Church, the General Council must meet. Venice and Vicenza were suggested as alternative venues, but to no avail until the town of Trent, in Italy but close to the Austrian border, proved acceptable to a majority of the parties. In 1544 Charles and Francis signed the Peace of Crèpy, Paul again convened the Council and in December 1545, despite Charles's opposition to its timing and to its agenda, the delegates at last assembled.

These delegates had to decide what sort of Church they wanted. Was it to be an exclusive institution with narrowly defined doctrines, imposing its uniformity with the utmost vigour, or was it to be a liberal, comprehensive organisation taking into account the pressures and changes of the age, and allowing for differences of opinion on minor issues, while requiring orthodoxy on the fundamental points? The events leading up to 1545 made it almost certain that the former view would be victorious. This is not to say that much that was liberal and 'modern' did not ultimately remain within the Church, but it did so securely only well away from Rome; the nearer to the Eternal City the greater was the atmosphere of austerity and severity which, especially during the pontificate of Carafa, dominated the papal court.

Such an austere atmosphere could not be permanent, and that it was accepted even temporarily, was due to the fear of the growth of Protestantism, a fear which also provoked the summoning of the General Council. Thus the Counter Reformation gradually became a reaction to Protestantism; nevertheless, initially, it had been a genuine reform movement with its roots in the Middle Ages, and stimulated by the problems and conditions of early sixteenth-century society.

Principal Events

The emergence of Luther

1517.	Ninety-five Propositions
1518.	Debate with Cajetan
1519.	Debate with Eck
1521.	Diet of Worms
	Excommunication of Luther

Early reforming and revivalists' groups

1494.	Oratory at Vicenza
1497.	St Catherine's Oratory at Genoa
1517.	Oratory of the Divine Love at Rome
1524.	Congregation of Clerks Regular (the Theatines)
1529.	Re-founding of the Capucins
1535.	Ursulines

The Jesuits

1491–1556.	Life of Loyola
1534.	Loyola and his friends take the initial vows in Paris
1540.	Jesuit Order officially accepted by Paul III
	Jesuit College founded in Rome
1545.	Jesuit College founded in Vienna
1555.	Jesuit College founded in Cologne
1556.	Jesuit College founded in Ingolstadt

Events immediately preceding Trent

1537.	*Consilium de Emendenda Ecclesia*
1541.	Ecclesiastical Meeting at Regensburg
1542.	Death of Contarini
	Roman Inquisition

PART IV
The Council of Trent

[12] THE FIRST SESSION, IMPERIAL DESIGNS FRUSTRATED

When the first session of the Council of Trent assembled in December 1545 it was hardly representative of the whole Roman Catholic Church; of 700 bishops eligible to attend only 31 were present at the opening ceremony. During the most productive periods, April and June 1546 and January and March 1547, the number varied between a minimum of 51 and a maximum of 62, who were joined by 40 or 50 theological and canon law experts, most of whom were friars. At the first session therefore the total average attendance was something in the region of 100.

This was of vital importance in directing the course which the Council would take, for with the Council meeting in Italy and with Francis I sending no representatives the Italian bishops were by far the majority. Although by no means every Italian bishop fully supported the Papacy – the bishops from Naples for example, owed allegiance to the Emperor Charles V – Italian domination of the Council did entail papal domination; thus fears of a revival of conciliar supremacy soon faded, particularly after the issue was raised and defeated early in the debates.

The first decisions taken at Trent concerned procedure, and these again favoured the Papacy. It was decided that three cardinals, del Monte, Cervini and Pole, appointed by Paul III to preside over the proceedings, were to nominate the subjects to be discussed and that discussions should initially take place amongst the theologians and the experts in canon law, with the bishops acting as silent onlookers. This was known as a 'particular congregation'. The conclusions reached in this 'particular congregation' then became the basis for further discussion by the bishops and heads of religious orders sitting alone, in what was called a 'general congregation'. The decisions of these 'general congregations' were drafted into a decree and the decrees were formally promulgated in a 'session' when the whole assembly met together in the cathedral of Trent. Papal approval was then needed, but this was unlikely to be withheld since the procedure dictated that the papal view prevailed.

There were, however, further safeguards for the Papacy. The practice at earlier Councils whereby voting was done by nations, was rejected at Trent, instead the bishops voted as individuals; furthermore there was to be no voting by proxy – a decision which greatly favoured the Italian majority.

Charles V, hoping before long to persuade the Lutherans to attend wanted the Council to deal initially with matters of discipline; having thus removed abuses about which Catholics and Protestants complained, he believed that a compromise could be reached which would restore the unity of Christendom. The Papacy, on the other hand, was anxious that the Council should quickly and firmly clarify Catholic doctrines. After considerable discussion it was decided, despite the protests of the Spanish and Neopolitan bishops, that matters of discipline and doctrine would be debated simultaneously; there was to be no attempt to re-state the whole of Catholic theology, only to deal with the issues raised by Protestant reformers, although no reformer was mentioned by name in the first session. This was a defeat for Charles V whose actions from then on, increasingly conflicted with the proceedings at Trent.

In his opening speech Cardinal Pole made it clear that the main burden of guilt for the Church's ills rested on the bishops; such self-criticism augured well for the future of the Council which at once concentrated on the task of re-defining the most controversial points of doctrine. The Council did abide by its decision to debate doctrinal and disciplinary questions at the same time, but for simplicity the doctrinal decisions will be considered first.

By 8 April 1546 the decree concerning the respective authority of the Scriptures and the Church's tradition had been prepared. In this the Council, rejecting the Protestant assertion that sole reliance should be placed on God's word as revealed in the Bible, decreed that

Following the example of the orthodox Fathers, this council receives and venerates, with equal pious affection and reverence, all the books both of the New and the Old Testaments, since one God is the author of both, together with the said Traditions, as well as those pertaining to faith as those pertaining to morals, as having been given either from the lips of Christ or by the dictation of the Holy Spirit and preserved by unbroken succession in the Catholic Church.

Since many different translations of the Bible had recently appeared the Council decided that the authorised version for Roman Catholics was St Jerome's Vulgate (Latin) edition, and it was categorically stated that 'to decide the true meaning and interpretation of the Holy Scriptures is the business of the Church'. Furthermore the Council declared its intention of instigating a thorough revision of the Roman Index. The effect of these decrees was not merely to refute Protestant teachings and to re-assert Catholic Doctrine but, more important, to confirm the authority of all the institutions of the Church, including the Papacy, in interpreting the Christian message. No room was left for Luther's individual interpretation, and little room for the mysticism of northern Europe. The only way to God for a Roman Catholic was through the Church.

These decrees had been arrived at only after considerable debate, but this was as nothing compared to the length of the debates which followed on original sin and justification. The Protestant view stressed man's original sin and depravity and his consequent inability to justify himself in the eyes of God; so conscious of man's sinful nature was Luther that he taught that only God could give him the power to overcome his own hopeless position. In the decree on original sin, published on 17 June

1546, the Catholics rejected this view. While accepting man's original sin, they decreed that Christ's sacrifice on the cross had obtained for men intrinsic merit of their own, and that by baptism and by participating in Christ's sacrifice at each celebration of the mass man could, by his own efforts, obtain more merit still. This was clearly a rejection of Luther's view of justification through faith alone, but before the decree on justification could be produced considerable arguments had to be met from within the Church itself.

The liberal Catholic view of Double Justification (see page 76) was discussed and rejected, but other differences remained. The Dominicans stressed the importance of God's grace in justifying man; the Jesuits, typically, wished the decree to lay more stress on man's ability to help himself, while the Augustinians at Trent were still prepared not only to stress the importance of God's grace but even to accept some limited form of predestination. Hence the discussions lasted from June 1546 through to the end of the year, by which time a decree was produced which held a balance amongst the Catholic views, although disputes continued, while utterly rejecting the Protestant views.

Luther had declared that there was nothing a man could do to bring about his own salvation; God alone, in his all seeing wisdom had predestined men, and to some men he had granted (imputed was the technical term) the ability to have true faith, to share truly in the sacraments and to do good works. In other words, good works were the result and not the cause of man receiving God's grace. Luther had therefore concluded that since he could do nothing, but since God had proved his love by sending his only son to die for mankind, he must simply trust in God's goodness and forgiveness.

The Council declared in January 1547, in nine pages of carefully worded Latin script, that God's grace was available both through man's faith and through his good works which included not only works of charity but, more important, participation in the Church's sacraments; in condemning the view 'that man's free will has been wholly lost and destroyed after Adam's sin' it confirmed man's ability to accept or reject God's offer of grace;

thus the more a man carried out good works the more merit, and therefore the more justification, he received. Justification was therefore available through a combination of man's good works and God's willingness to grant him grace.

Since the decrees on original sin and on justification stressed the importance of participation in the sacraments it was essential to answer Luther's contention that only baptism and communion were genuine. This was done in March 1547 with a decree in which the Council followed traditional Catholic teaching by accepting seven sacraments; baptism, penance, marriage, ordination, the eucharist, (celebration of the mass), confirmation and divine unction. Although further discussions were held on baptism and confirmation the vexed question of transubstantiation in the mass was held over for another occasion.

By March 1547 therefore the Roman Catholic Church had dealt with some of the most disputed points of doctrine, but no more was to be achieved in this first session, for in May 1547 plague appeared in Trent and, without specific papal approval, the Council decided to move south to Bologna. This movement brought to a head the worsening relations between the Emperor Charles V and Paul III.

In 1544 Charles V had signed the Peace of Crèpy with Francis I, thereby freeing himself to deal with his German problems. He aimed not only to reduce the princes as a political threat but to summon a conference which, having reached a religious compromise for Germany, would enable him to persuade the Lutherans to attend the Council of Trent; in this his hopes were dashed when the meeting at Passau in February 1546 was ruined by the non-attendance of the Lutherans. Charles therefore prepared for war.

Despite his disappointment at the orthodoxy of the doctrinal decrees issuing from Trent, Charles signed a treaty with Paul III in June 1546, by which Paul agreed to provide men and money for the German war. Meanwhile Charles attempted, with considerable success, to neutralise the leading German Protestant princes, Maurice of Saxony and Philip of Hesse. In the war which followed Charles suffered initial setbacks but, by a victory over the Schmalkaldic League at Ingolstadt in August 1546, most of southern Germany fell under his control, a domination confirmed in April 1547 by an even greater victory at Mühlberg. Germany seemed to be at Charles's feet and, at last, he was in a position to force the Lutherans to attend the Council.

Nevertheless Charles was unable to impede the decisions being taken at Trent, and the highly orthodox decree on justification, published in January 1547, infuriated him; in that same month Paul withdrew his contingent from Charles's army, supposedly because of plague and the final blow came when the Council moved to Bologna in May 1547. Charles could never be persuaded that Paul had not engineered the move in order to retain control of the council.

It now seemed to Charles that Paul III was intent on placing every obstacle in the way of the compromise which Charles so desired. The imperial ambassador denounced Paul to his face, Charles declared that he would 'save the Catholic Church in spite of the Holy See', and ordered his thirteen bishops not to move to Bologna but to stay at Trent. This they did, and Charles considered them the true Council but no one moved to join them so nothing was achieved.

Meanwhile in May 1548 he produced the Interim of Augsburg, which he hoped would satisfy Lutherans in Germany and which would serve as the starting point for further discussions. Two major concessions were granted; the wine might be given to the laity in the mass and priests were allowed to marry. This not only failed to satisfy the Lutherans, but served to enrage the Papacy, to whom it seemed that Charles had set himself up as a rival authority; nevertheless in return for these concessions Charles demanded that the Lutherans should attend the Council.

The political situation was so confused, and the Council so divided, that nothing was achieved during the latter part of 1547 or throughout 1548 either at Bologna or at Trent; this being the case, Paul recognised the inevitable and allowed the bishops to return home in September 1549, thus ending the first session. Paul, himself, barely outlived his Council.

Throughout the session he had quarrelled with Charles V, not only over the decisions reached at Trent and Charles's intentions in Germany but also over his family's position in Parma and Piacenza which, since 1545, had been ruled by his son Pierluigi. Charles sought to establish his own influence in the area and when, in 1547, Pierluigi was murdered, his son Ottavio held Charles responsible and prepared to re-open the wars in Italy against the Emperor. This, together with his other problems and old age, helped to break Paul who died in November 1549 at the age of 81.

Despite his worldliness and his manifest faults, Paul was one of the most significant popes in the history of the Roman Catholic Church. By summoning the General Council to Trent, by appointing reformers to high positions, by encouraging men to work for reform, to found societies and to investigate the faults of the Church, Paul was the first to give that leadership without the Catholic Church could never had rejuvenated itself.

The first session did extremely important but less disputed work upon discipline and morality, beginning in 1546, with a discussion on education. One school of thought, including Cervini and Pole, hoped that the education given to priests would in future be centred on biblical studies, as More, Fisher and Erasmus had suggested. This, they thought, would lead to a greater understanding of Christ's teaching. Had the proposals been accepted they might have considerably changed the character of the priesthood, but they were not, and the traditional scholastic education was retained, illustrating once more the reactionary nature of the Council.

The actual decree on education, promulgated in June 1546, ordered that every cathedral and town should possess a priest capable of instruction, but in this and in other provisions of the decree there was little that was either new or of great significance. On the other hand, a decree on preaching did produce the beginnings of important changes. Having established that 'preaching is the chief of all a bishop's duties', and that parish priests should preach on all feast days and Sundays, the responsibility for enforcing this was left with the bishop who received greater control over sermons preached by friars in his diocese. In addition, automatic penalties were laid down for failures to comply with this decree. This was the start of that process by which the Council, entrusting greater responsibility and more power to the bishops, produced the efficiency which characterised the Counter Reformation Church.

In January 1547 the Council issued a decree which further strengthened the bishop's hold over his diocese. In attempting to end pluralism and absenteeism, however, it failed. The argument hinged on whether divine law insisted that bishops should be resident, but no solution was reached and, although pluralism and absenteeism were condemned and automatic penalties devised, little was achieved. The penalties, involving loss of revenue, were not sufficient deterrent and in any case nothing was done to prevent the granting of papal dispensations. Thus the problem was shelved, to be re-opened in bitter debate in the third session. One important issue, significantly, was not debated, during the first session. Despite Luther's attack on papal supremacy, the Council took the pope's leadership for granted, and the Papacy emerged stronger than ever.

Upon the death of Paul III, Cardinal del Monte, one of the legates at the first session, was elected Julius III (1549–54). Julius, who made his reputation as an administrator and as a canon lawyer, although a believer in reform, was not energetic, and during his years of office he occasionally relapsed into the worldly existence of earlier popes. Nor was he ever strong willed enough to be totally independent of the European princes. Nevertheless, he did send Pole to England in 1553 to help in the restoration of the Catholic faith; he did, although unsuccessfully, attempt a reform of the Dataria (the papal office which dispensed favours in return for cash) and, most important, in December 1550, he summoned the Council to meet again at Trent.

Charles V hoped that the German Protestants would attend this session and so, with reservations, he gave it his support. Henry II of France, on the other hand, was at loggerheads with the Papacy fearing above all a settlement which would ease the Emperor's problems in Germany, and consequently no French delegate attended; indeed, it appeared for a while as if the French Church might break altogether with the Papacy. That it did not do so was largely due to the conciliatory influence of Cardinal Guise of Lorraine. Meanwhile Henry prepared to re-open the war with Charles, further irked by the fact that Julius refused to join him. In this unpromising atmosphere the Council began; once again the attendance of less than fifty bishops was disappointingly low.

The legates appointed to preside over this session were the Archbishop of Siponto, the Bishop of Verona and Cardinal Crescenzi who was the senior and most important. A firm believer in papal supremacy, and in the need to reaffirm traditional Catholic teaching in the face of reforming ideas, Crescenzi was unlikely to offer conciliation to the German Protestants, who did not arrive until January 1552 and the Council decided therefore to deal first with the sacraments, particularly penance, extreme unction and the mass.

Preliminary work had already been done in the first session, and decrees reaffirming the orthodox Catholic position were promulgated, of which the most important was that of October 1551 concerning transubstantiation. This condemned Protestant reformers, who rejected the magical change of the bread and wine into Christ's body and blood during the mass, stating categorically that:

Since, Christ our Redeemer said that that which he offered under the appearance of bread was truly his body, it has therefore always been held in the Church of God, and this holy Council now declares anew, that through consecration of the bread and wine there comes about a conversion of the whole substance of the bread into the substance of the body of Christ our Lord and of the whole substance of the wine into the substance of his blood. And this conversion is by the Holy Catholic Church conveniently and properly called transubstantiation.

and

If any one shall deny that the body and blood of our Lord Jesus Christ together with his spirit and divinity, to wit, Christ all in all, are not truly and materially contained in the holy sacrament of the Eucharist, and shall assert that the Eucharist is but a symbol or figure, let him be anathema.

The question of the sacrifice in the mass was deferred but, as far as those hoping for conciliation were concerned, the damage was done. The Lutherans, arriving in January 1552, three months after the decree on transubstantiation, made three fundamental demands: that they should sit in the Council equal in authority with the Catholics, that the Council should have the power to decide matters over the head of the pope and that all decisions so far taken should be null and void. The Council announced that it would consider these suggestions, but this truly was the end of compromise for neither the Papacy nor the Council was prepared to accede to these demands; thus the permanent breach between Catholics and Protestants was revealed. In a negative way this was the real achievement of the second session, for never again were there high level suggestions from either side that compromise or conciliation were possible.

The political situation now determined that the second session should end. War had broken out in Germany in March 1552 and the Emperor, forced out of Germany by a combination of German princes backed by France, fled through Austria towards Trent; since the city seemed in danger the Council dissolved itself in April 1552. For Charles this was virtually the end, and affairs in Germany were handed over to his brother Ferdinand who made the political settlement at Augsburg in 1555, by which each prince was allowed to choose either Roman Catholicism or Lutheranism for his state. The Papacy disapproved of the settlement but was powerless to prevent it, and so when the Council next met it did so in the knowledge that Germany was legally divided over religion.

In fact the Council did not meet again for almost ten years, the long interval being due to the fact that from 1555 to 1559 Carafa occupied the papal throne as Paul IV. Carafa had not been the first choice as successor to Julius, who died in 1555, but Cardinal Cervini, who was elected as Marcellus II outlived his election by only twenty days and so the conclave turned to Carafa, partly because of his seniority, and partly because it was felt that, after the lethargic latter days of Julius, a more vigorous attitude was required.

Paul IV

Carafa had never believed in the necessity of a General Council, taking the view that the Church could be put in order by strict appliance of the canon law and by firm leadership. As Pope, despite his advancing years, he proceeded to put his beliefs into practice.

By forceful use of the Inquisition the city of Rome and the Papal Curia were purged. In August 1558 over 100 wandering monks and friars were rounded up and sent either to prison or to the papal galleys; over 100 bishops who lingered around the papal court hoping for favours were ordered back to their dioceses; the seemingly impossible job of reforming the Dataria was taken up where Julius III had left off, and was successfully completed. For four years Carafa's iron rule showed no mercy to clerics or lay people of whatever rank and, although his methods were dictatorial and often excessively severe, they were effective.

In some ways, however, Carafa's rule endangered the whole future of the Counter Reformation for as an ardent Italian nationalist he despised all things Spanish. Only the death of Loyola and the election in 1556 of Lainez as General prevented him disbanding the Jesuits; moreover, in 1557 he encouraged Henry II to drive the Spanish from Italy, thereby re-opening the Italian Wars which, by the Peace of Cateau Cambresis two years later, left Spain's hold on Italy stronger than ever. In addition to involving the Papacy in international politics he angered many by his severity. Cardinal Morone was imprisoned for criticising the persecutions which he saw in Rome, while the comparatively liberal Cardinal Pole, having been deprived of his legateship, was only spared further papal wrath by his absence in England. Such treatment was beneficial only in small doses, however, and it was to the benefit of the Church that Carafa died in 1559.

[14] THE THIRD SESSION AND THE SIGNIFICANCE OF THE COUNCIL

On the death of Carafa a member of the Medici family (not the Florentine branch) was elected Pius IV. Although possessing few outstanding qualities Pius was experienced and level-headed; he maintained Carafa's attack on abuses within the Curia, although he had little time for Carafa's family whose ambitions he ruined, and he introduced as his private secretary Carlo Borromeo, later to become one of the outstanding figures of the Counter Reformation. His greatest service, however, was to reconvene the Council.

It was the French situation which, above all, convinced Pius of the need to act. During the 1550s Calvinism made such progress – it was estimated that ten per cent of Frenchmen were already Calvinists – that the government, headed by the politically inexperienced Catherine de Medici, summoned a religious meeting to Poissy in 1561. Pius feared that Catherine was on the brink of a separate settlement with the Protestants which might diminish Catholic influence in France.

In Germany, where both Calvinism and Lutheranism continued to make headway, Emperor Ferdinand I was also pressing that more concessions be given; Pius hoped therefore, that a third session of the Council might act as a rallying point. The opening was timed for 1561, but since only 9 bishops were present, it was delayed until January 1562, when 113 bishops attended, of whom 86 were Italian, 13 Spanish and none French, since the French delegation, led by Cardinal Guise of Lorraine, did not arrive until November.

Such was the turmoil at the beginning of the session, that it seemed unlikely that this would prove to be the most constructive of the three sessions. Prompted by Philip II, who objected to papal power growing any stronger, the Spanish bishops pressed that the authority of the Papacy should be discussed, suggesting even that bishops were the equals of the pope. On the other hand, the Spanish faction did accept the decisions of the first two sessions, whereas both the French and Imperial delegations wanted them nullified, so that the third session would constitute an entirely new Council which could offer concessions to the Protestants. Faced with such basic differences, and with no prospect of progress, Pius IV despatched Cardinal Morone as an additional legate, to find some way out of the confusion.

Morone, in constant touch with Borromeo in Rome, realised that since the nations were divided he might be able to make separate terms with each. Consequently he journeyed to Innsbruck where he offered Ferdinand various concessions, the most attractive of which was support for Ferdinand's son, Maximilian, to be elected King of the Romans and heir to the Empire; thereafter Ferdinand agreed to cooperate. Morone won over Cardinal Guise by offering him a position in the debates equal in authority to the other legates; thereafter the danger of French secession from the Council receded. With the opposition of the French and the Imperialists overcome there was little that Spain could do, and the way was open for Morone to introduce his programme of reform for the Council to consider. It was never specifically stated that the decisions of the first two sessions remained in force but this was taken for granted; neither France nor Ferdinand raising further objections.

Morone's programme formed the basis for the reforms which followed, the most important of which was the establishment of colleges in every diocese for the training of young priests; an

ignorant lower clergy had been one of the greatest faults of the
medieval Church and, although it took time to implement, this
decree had enormous impact in shaping the Church of the future.
Another decree dealt with the problem of clandestine marriages
– those not carried out in church, where the two partners took
their vows privately. The Council accepted that the vows
taken were the actual sacrament, but ordered that all marriages
should take place in the presence of a priest and two witnesses;
marriages carried out in secret were declared illegal, hence the
authority of the Church as the only institution through which
marriages could be solemnised was further strengthened.

The assembly then turned its attention to points of doctrine
which had come under fire from the Protestants, but, as in the
first two sessions, no concessions were made. The existence of
purgatory and the usefulness of indulgences was confirmed,
although it was decreed that indulgences were no longer to be
sold; celibacy for priests was upheld and the desirability of a
true veneration of the saints re-stated; on the question of a
sacrifice in the mass the Jesuits and the Dominicans quarrelled
bitterly, but traditional Catholic teaching was affirmed, that at
each celebration Christ's body was sacrificed for mankind.

The decree which caused the most debate in the third session,
and which was second in importance only to that establishing
colleges in every diocese, concerned the duties and obligations
of bishops. The delegates argued whether divine law stated that
bishops must reside in their dioceses or whether the Pope could
grant dispensations excusing them from doing so. This raised
the issue of whether a bishop derived his authority from God or
from the pope, but, although the Spanish delegation favoured
the former view, in the end these contentious issues were side
stepped and no decision reached. Pluralism and absenteeism
were forbidden; the bishop was ordered above all to superintend
his diocese and no papal dispensations were to be allowed without
the bishop's knowledge. Thus more responsibility was given to
the bishops, but along with that responsibility they received
greater authority.

Attempts were made to discuss other topics and to place

formal obligation on the princes to enforce the decrees, but in
the end the Council contented itself with requesting the Papacy
to prepare a revised Index (carried out in 1564 and completed
in 1596), Catechism (1566), Breviary (1568) and Missal (1570).
Morone, fearing that further strife was about to break out then
hurried the session to a conclusion. On 4 December 1563 the
Council dissolved itself, thus ending the last council until 1869.
In January 1564 Pius IV confirmed its decrees.

Although many Catholics disagreed with the decisions taken
at Trent there could no longer be confusion over main issues; by
clarifying doctrine and by tightening discipline the Council gave
a lead which inspired Catholics throughout the world – as such
it was the focal point of the Counter Reformation. Nor is it true
to say that the Council was the cause of the final breach with
the Protestants, for Luther and Calvin challenged too much that
was fundamental, and unless the Church had been prepared to
depart radically from traditional practices no compromise was
possible. Trent, therefore, merely accepted a schism which could
not be healed.

Although Trent helped to create the modern Roman Catholic
Church – in the sense that its doctrine and structure lasted until
recent times – the decisions taken were extremely conservative.
Faced with the bitter truth that it no longer represented the
universal Church the Council, turning its back on the ideas of
even its own liberals, accepted the need to define its doctrine
more closely than ever before. The education of the clergy
remained traditional, little heed being paid to the advances in
Biblical studies by Catholic humanists. Moreover, no provision
was made for the laity to participate in administration, and
although mysticism was not specifically condemned, the Trent
decrees clearly implied that man could find God only through the
institutions of the established Church. Within that organisation
the pope, without whose pressure (exerted through the legates)
little would have been achieved, emerged supreme and theories
of conciliar supremacy disappeared.

Philip II complained that his bishops had gone to the Council
as bishops and returned as parish priests but, in fact, the greatest

innovation at Trent concerned the increase in their authority. Pole had set the tone in his opening speech to the first session, thus the obligation for keeping the Church pure and disciplined, was placed on the bishops as never before.

Partly as a result of Trent where, of 270 bishops who attended 187 were Italian, and partly because of the growth of Protestantism elsewhere, the Church became increasingly Italian in character, and since the Council no foreigner has been elected Pope.

Much had therefore been achieved, but much remained to be done. The more difficult task of enforcing the decrees rested not merely with the Papacy and the various orders, but with the secular rulers. France did not ratify the decrees until 1615; Philip II did so in 1565, but with considerable reservations and although Portugal, the Emperor and the south of Switzerland accepted them at once, the German Diet utterly refused to do so. Consequently much depended upon the attitude of the princes and on the characters of future popes.

Principal Events

The First Session of Trent, December 1545–September 1549

1546.	April.	Decree on Scripture and Tradition
		St Jerome's Bible accepted as the Authorised Version
	June.	Decrees on Education and Preaching
		Decree on Original Sin
	August.	Charles V defeats the German Protestants at Ingolstadt
1547.	January.	Decree on the Duties of Bishops
		Decree on Justification
	March.	Decree on the Seven Sacraments
	April.	Charles V defeats the German Protestants at Muhlberg
	May.	The Council moves to Bologna
1548.	May.	Charles V grants the Interim of Augsburg

The Second Session of Trent, May 1551–April 1552

1551.	October.	Decree on Transubstantiation
1552.	January.	Arrival of the Lutherans
	March.	Renewal of war in Germany
1555.		Abdication of Charles V
		Peace of Augsburg for Germany

The Third Session of Trent, January 1562–December 1563

1563.	Decree establishing Seminaries in each Diocese
	Decree against Clandestine Marriages
	Decrees confirming Purgatory, Indulgences and the Veneration of the Saints
	Decree confirming Celibacy of Priests
	Decree confirming the Sacrifice in the Mass
	Decree on the Duties of Bishops

PART V
The Reformed Papacy

[15] THE TRIUMPH OF LEADERSHIP

The Church was extremely fortunate that the first man to be
elected pope after the Council of Trent was the epitome of the
Counter Reformation. Michele Ghislieri, a Dominican, who took
the name of Pius V (1566–72), was the last pope to be canonised.
In his saintly life and in his dedication to the progress of the
Church he set himself the highest standards of personal discipline, spending entire weeks in meditation. His ascetic ideals
had a great impact. The cardinals were forbidden to eat off
silver and the expenses of the court were cut by half; he made
bishops' residence in their sees compulsory and he introduced
strict regulations for the observance of Sundays, children in
Rome having to attend church on Sunday afternoons to learn
of the Christian faith. Considerable use was made of the Inquisition and the Catechism (1566), the Breviary (1568) and the
Missal (1570) were revised as the Council had directed.

So devoted to the extension of Roman Catholicism was Pius
that he attempted to forward it throughout Europe, but he was
no diplomat and rarely did he achieve his aims. He excommunicated Elizabeth of England in 1570 and supported Mary,
Queen of Scots, with money; in the Netherlands he encouraged
Philip II's policy of religious persecution and in France he
exhorted Charles IX to take action against the Huguenots; in
none of these countries, however, did he pay sufficient attention
to practical politics, so that his policies led to bloodshed and to
a growth of religious hatred. On the other hand he sank his

differences with Spain and Venice to form the Holy League, whose fleet defeated the Turks at Lepanto in 1571.

Gregory XIII (1572–85), an ex-professor of Law at Bologna University, was equally determined that the Church should remain pure and that the decrees of Trent should be enforced, but he lacked the strictness and harshness of Pius. Although a gentler character, he was an energetic figure who achieved much of a practical nature; as befitted an ex-university professor he was interested in education, re-founding the Jesuit College in Rome and spending considerable sums of money on other religious institutions. On the administrative side he created more nuncios to the European princes, thus encouraging them to enforce Trent, and he set up committees in Rome to regulate the Index and to oversee episcopal affairs. Furthermore, since so much emphasis had been placed on the work of the bishops, he risked a clash with the secular rulers by insisting that all men appointed to bishoprics should be properly qualified. Gregory is best remembered, however, for an act less concerned with the well being of the Church. He was responsible for a reform of the calendar which still bears his name.

Sixtus V (1585–90), a Franciscan whose family name was Peretti and who came from humble origins, was a man of energy and ability whom some see as the greatest pope of the period. On the other hand he is often accused of excessive ambition and of reviving abuses such as the sale of offices. He was undoubtedly a man of vision who saw his main task as that of restoring order and prosperity to the Papal States, which latterly had returned to their former unruly condition. A building programme was undertaken and much of the impressive side of the city including a new road system, new water supplies and an enlargement of the Vatican library, dates from this period. Probably more important though, was his encouragement of agriculture, commerce and industries such as wool and silk, whereby Rome became, once more, a prosperous and better ordered city, although much remained to be done.

Sixtus also improved the administration of the Church, initiating several important reforms. He fixed the number of

cardinals at seventy and established fifteen permanent committees to deal with papal business (see page 105) while, within
the Curia, he promoted an interest in science and in education
in general – personally revising the Vulgate text of St Jerome's
Bible. In foreign affairs he encouraged Philip II to launch the
Armada against England, he supervised the Church's work in
Poland and he approached Henry of Navarre in France in the
hope of his reconversion to Roman Catholicism.

Three Popes followed Sixtus in quick succession. Urban VII
(1590), Gregory XIV (1590–1) and Innocent IX (1591) were all
likely to have carried on the work of reform but none of them
lived long enough, and the Church had to wait for the peaceful
and devout Clement VIII (1592–1605) before a constructive
policy could be resumed. Clement, from the Aldobrandini
family, paid particular attention to the appointment of bishops
and cardinals, ensuring, wherever possible, that suitable men
were selected; he watched equally carefully for corruption
within the Curia, he revised the Index, supported the Inquisition
and completed the final revision of the Breviary.

Above all, however, Clement was a peacemaker. Within the
Church he tried to reconcile the Jesuits and the Dominicans
and, towards the European nations also, he assumed a more
peaceful policy. Having received Henry of Navarre back into
the Catholic faith and recognised him as King of France, he
helped negotiate the Peace of Vervins between France and Spain
in 1598; in this way he acquired the friendship of the French
monarchy, thereby freeing the Papacy from reliance on Spain, a
development quickly appreciated by the rest of Europe. Nor
did he continue the aggressive policy towards England; instead
believing that peaceful methods were more likely to benefit
Catholicism, he patronised schools for English and Scottish
missionaries. Although little of spectacular note was achieved,
Clement's rule was a period of quiet consolidation and development.

Reform in Italy

Thus in the decades following the Council of Trent the improvement in the moral standards of the Papacy was maintained; moreover, within Italy, especially within the Papal States, it had become more powerful. There, the decrees had been enforced, bishops and cardinals carefully selected, the administrative machinery of the Church overhauled and law, order and magnificent buildings brought to Rome itself. Since the 1560s, however, there had been quarrels over other matters of papal jurisdiction. Philip II who, until his death in 1598, controlled Sicily, Naples and Milan opposed papal pretensions in his territories. Consequently, although, like his father, he failed to introduce the Spanish Inquisition, he kept a tight hold over the Church in Naples and Sicily, where he retained the power to appoint the bishops and to prevent the publication of papal bulls.

In Milan even more difficulties arose when Philip's governors, the Duke of Alburquerque and Requensens, clashed with the energetic Carlo Borromeo, Archbishop from 1565 to 1585. Borromeo, while enforcing the decrees of Trent, published the bull *In doena domini* which forbade princes to levy further taxes on their subjects. Spain retaliated by mobilising troops, whereupon Borromeo cursed the governor, Alburquerque, but neither Spain nor the Papacy could afford to quarrel for long over such an important area as Milan, and the affair was soon patched up; in practical terms, however, Borromeo was able to continue with his work. In fact, Philip and the popes of the period had good cause to cooperate. A mutual fear of the Turks and Philip's desire to retain his right to tax the Church in Spain ensured that, even while quarrels were going on, there was an underlying cooperation.

To a lesser extent the same was true of the one independent power in Italy, the republic of Venice. Before Lepanto in 1571 Venice often sank her differences with both Spain and the Papacy in order to ward off the Turkish threat but, in the long run, she opposed papal interference as much as did Spain. Thus by the late sixteenth century, with the fear of the Turks diminished, she began to pursue a different policy. She looked more to France for friendship and in 1605 she challenged the papal attack on her right to control her own clergy. This led to a complete breach in which the Church of Venice was placed under an interdict, but, although a compromise was quickly worked out, Venice won her point and the fundamental differences of opinion remained.

These quarrels, however, were of a political nature. On questions concerning the health of the Church, the Papacy received more cooperation. The Roman Inquisition eradicated all traces of Protestantism and the decrees of Trent were generally enforced, although their uncompromising spirit, exemplified in the Index, the Inquisition and the work of the popes in Rome, manifested itself in the various states in different ways. Most varieties of Protestantism had appeared in Italy – there had even been an Anabaptist synod at Venice in 1550 – but these were successfully dealt with. The free intellectual atmosphere of the Renaissance was smothered, however, particularly in Naples, where popular festivals were combined with the ceremonial burning of dangerous literature, and in Milan where Borromeo purified the Church and its clergy.

Venice alone escaped because of its political independence, and it is significant that during the late sixteenth century, when the Index and Inquisition stifled most of Italy, she experienced her High Renaissance. This did not prevent the Counter Reformation entering Venice, however, and a string of notable reformers from Contarini onwards emerged, but with a more liberal spirit. The Venetian Senate maintained its control of episcopal appointments and the clergy remained predominantly Venetian, thereby ensuring that the Counter Reformation there retained a highly national character.

Meanwhile the orders continued to exert considerable influence, the Jesuits, in particular, expanding their work. With colleges already founded at Bologna (1546), Messina (1548), Palermo (1549) and Rome (1550) they toured the states drawing large crowds and gaining followers and converts from all sections of Italian society, including the Farnese family, Cardinal Morone and, perhaps most important of all, Carlo Borromeo to

whom Ribera introduced the Spiritual Exercises in 1562 while
he was secretary to Pius IV. No man so symbolised the spirit of
the Counter Reformation in Italy as the saintly but austere
Borromeo yet his was a Jesuit influence, indeed Jesuit ideas
permeated the whole movement except perhaps in Venice.

Thus by the end of the sixteenth century the Church, faced
with the growth of Protestantism elsewhere, had at least
secured its hold on Italy. This was achieved at considerable cost,
however, for the uncompromising spirit of the Index, the
Inquisition and the decrees of Trent, together with the continual
presence of Spain, deprived Italy of both its intellectual and
political freedom.

Administrative reforms

Throughout the period after Trent the Papacy implemented
important administrative changes, of which the most pressing
were those concerned with its sources of revenue. Since the
1520s the Church had found itself in financial difficulties as parts
of Europe, having accepted Protestantism, refused to pay their
dues to Rome. This serious loss of income played a large role in
prompting the Papacy to initiate reform but, as the sixteenth
century progressed, it became clear that some losses of income
were permanent and that other sources must be found. This was
done mainly through greater attention to the Papal States
whose economy was improved, but whose prosperity was more
heavily taxed. In addition, the Papacy borrowed heavily in
Florence, especially in Genoa and in Rome where something
akin to a national debt arose; thus the Church relied more on its
Italian resources which increased its Italian appearance.

Gradually, although in an unspectacular fashion, the abuses
of the fifteenth and early sixteenth centuries were removed
from the Papal Curia, the best example being the purging of the
Dataria in the 1550s by Paul IV. To raise the moral tone, however, was not sufficient. If the Church hoped to make its voice
heard its administration had to be made more efficient.

Although, during the Middle Ages, the cardinals had often

tried to limit papal authority, the majority had resided in Rome and participated in the various congregations which had been established to handle the Church's affairs. In 1564 Pius IV added a congregation to deal with questions arising from the decrees of Trent; Gregory XIII set up congregations to look into reform of ceremonial and the canon law while Pius V formed a congregation for German affairs. These additions, and the growing complexity of papal business, required a wholesale reform of the system, involving both cardinals and congregations, which was largely achieved by Sixtus V who, in 1588, limited the number of cardinals to seventy and laid down precise qualifications for those holding the office. He then established fifteen permanent congregations to deal with such aspects of papal business as the appointment of bishops, the administration of the Papal States and the Inquisition. Each congregation was headed by a group of three to five cardinals, acting as heads of department and once a week the full consistory of cardinals met the pope to discuss the Church's business. Thus the central administration was brought into line with developments in civil government, although as yet few nations could rival such an organisation.

As time passed more congregations were added, the most important being the Congregation for the Propagation of the Faith, establishing in 1622 to coordinate the Church's missionary work. Furthermore, great care was taken in the selection of new cardinals who played such an important role in papal affairs. With these developments in the administration the office of Papal Secretary increased in significance, especially under Pius IV, to whom his nephew Borromeo was secretary, and under Pius V; moreover, it became standard practice for a relation of the pope to hold the position since a considerable degree of trust between the two men was essential.

The Papacy had possessed resident nuncios in countries such as Spain, Portugal, France, Austria and other Italian states for some time, but elsewhere the practice had been to send a nuncio only to carry out a specific task. As the Church attempted to recover ground lost to the Protestants, however, it became essential that closer relations should be maintained with the

Catholic princes. Gregory XIII therefore expanded the system by establishing resident nuncios at Brussels, at Cologne, at Salzburg and in Bavaria and Styria, whose work was controlled by the Congregation for the Propagation of the Faith in Rome.

The Roman Inquisition, founded in 1542, became more firmly established after Trent and, although it was never used effectively elsewhere, in Italy it had enormous impact, together with the Index which was revised at the instructions of the Council in 1564 and completed by Clement VIII in 1596. In addition, the Vatican set up its own printing press in 1587, an important acquisition in the paper war against heresy, but one which came surprisingly late.

Thus the Roman Catholic Church modernized itself for the task of combating both heresy and apathy. By the dogmatic definition of its doctrine, by the discipline imposed upon its clergy and by the confirmation of papal supremacy, a rigorous but narrow organisation was created. Moreover the Church ensured that a line of conscientious popes enforced the decrees of Trent and overhauled the administration at Rome. Nevertheless the Papacy could only directly be effective in Italy; thus, as the seventeenth century progressed, successive popes were forced to accept that elsewhere religious affairs depended increasingly upon the attitude of the ruling prince.

Leo XI (1605), a Medici, ruled only briefly but his successor, Paul V (1605–21), from the Borghese family, held office for the longest period since Paul III, and at a most difficult time. As the nations of Europe entered a period of general war so the progress of Roman Catholicism passed largely beyond the control of the Papacy, which could exert little influence except through societies such as the Jesuits or where the ruler himself was a devout Catholic. Consequently, although Paul was deeply involved in European affairs, his main achievements, and those of the popes who succeeded him, were limited to Italy, and, in particular, to Rome.

Paul advanced the fortunes of his own family and, like the Rennaissance popes was interested in the buildings of Rome – during his rule the main building of St Peter's was completed.

On the other hand he was a devout man who, without being an outstanding figure, served the Church well. The liturgical books were revised, the *Rituale Romanum* produced and the decrees of Trent enforced although understandably with the passage of time, not in the vigorous fashion of some of his predecessors.

In his short reign Gregory XV (1621-3) displayed considerable energy in encouraging the expansion of the Catholic faith. In 1622 he established the congregation for the Propagation of the Faith to supervise missionary work overseas (see page 159) but above all, he supported with money and advice Emperor Ferdinand II and Maximilian of Bavaria in their successful reconquest of Bohemia and the Palatinate. Despite this, however, papal influence over European affairs continued to diminish, and this became abundantly clear during the long reign of Urban VIII (1623-44).

Urban founded a printing press in Rome to assist missionary activities overseas and, as a patron of the arts, he continued the re-building of Rome, employing Bernini to apply the finishing touches to St Peter's. His principal work, however, was in the diplomatic field where he attempted to pursue a constructive policy throughout the wars which dominated the period of his rule. In these wars, religion was only one of many issues and Urban found himself faced with a situation in which Catholic France allied with Protestants against the Catholic Hapsburgs, who were themselves political rivals of the Papacy in Italy. Urban therefore attempted to conciliate between Bourbon and Hapsburg but in this he failed, and at no stage of the Thirty Years War was he able to exert any effective influence on the participants. Nor was his successor, Innocent X (1644-55), whose condemnation of the settlement made at Westphalia in 1648 went unheeded, and whose offer of help to Henrietta Maria in England proved worthless.

The truth was that although the Papacy emerged from Trent stronger than ever within the Church, it had become predominantly an Italian institution. This, together with the rise of national monarchies, the permanent establishment of Protestantism in parts of Europe and, particularly in the seventeenth century, the decline in religious fervour, seriously diminished its ability to affect international affairs. Nevertheless, by their enforcement of the Trent decrees, by their patronage of the Jesuits and other societies, and by their encouragement of the Catholic princes, the popes provided a lead in the struggle against heresy without which much of the success in France, the Netherlands, Germany and eastern Europe could not have been achieved.

Principal Events

The Popes

1550s.		Reform of the Dataria
1566–72.	Pius V	
1572–85.	Gregory XIII	
1585–90.	Sixtus V	
1588.		Limitation of the number of cardinals to 70
		15 permanent Congregations established to handle papal business
1590.	Urban VII	
1590–1.	Gregory XIV	
1591.	Innocent IX	
1592–1605.	Clement VIII	
1605.	Leo XI	
1605–21.	Paul V	
1621–3.	Gregory XV	
1622.		Congregation for the Propagation of the Faith established
1623–44.	Urban VIII	
1644–55.	Innocent X	

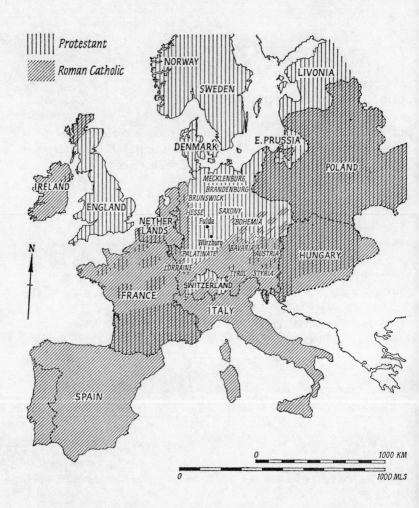

NORWAY

SWEDEN

LIVONIA

DENMARK

E. PRUSSIA

POLAND

MECKLENBURG,
BRANDENBURG

IRELAND

ENGLAND

NETHER-
LANDS

BRUNSWICK

HESSE   SAXONY
Fulda   BOHEMIA
Würzburg

PALATINATE   BAVARIA   AUSTRIA

HUNGARY

LORRAINE

TYROL   STYRIA

N

FRANCE

SWITZERLAND

ITALY

SPAIN

0   1000 KM

0   1000 MLS

THE RELIGIONS OF EUROPE c. 1570

*No outline map can provide a fully accurate picture of European religions.
These maps, therefore, are intended as a rough guide to illustrate the success*

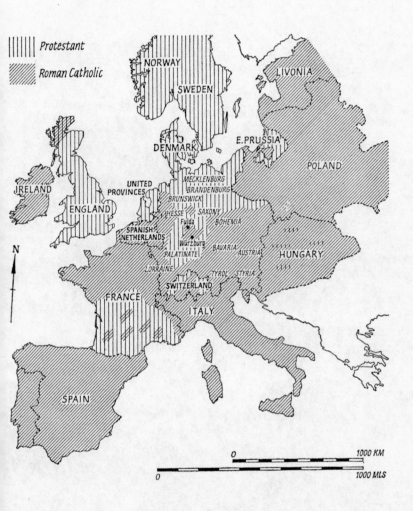

| | Protestant |
| | Roman Catholic |

NORWAY

SWEDEN

LIVONIA

DENMARK

E. PRUSSIA

IRELAND

UNITED PROVINCES

MECKLENBURG

BRANDENBURG

POLAND

ENGLAND

BRUNSWICK

HESSE   SAXONY

Fulda   BOHEMIA

SPANISH NETHERLANDS

Würzburg

N

PALATINATE   BAVARIA   AUSTRIA

HUNGARY

LORRAINE

TYROL   STYRIA

SWITZERLAND

FRANCE

ITALY

SPAIN

0 _____ 1000 KM

0 _____ 1000 MLS

THE RELIGIONS OF EUROPE 1648

*of the Counter Reformation between the middle decades of the sixteenth
century and the Westphalia settlement of 1648*

PART VI
The Counter Reformation
in Action

[16] WESTERN EUROPE

Through her spiritual influence and her political activities Spain became the power house of the Counter Reformation. Charles V (1516–56) and his son Philip II (1556–98) continued the processes begun by Ferdinand and Isabella (see page 46), by which the Church was brought increasingly under royal control and a stricter discipline enforced upon the clergy and the religious orders. Seeing the growth of heresy in northern Europe – especially in Germany – and fearing its influence on Spain the government began to investigate anything which seemed to endanger the purity of Spain's religious life. Two movements caused particular concern.

As in other parts of Europe a reaction against the elaborate ceremony of the Church produced mystical groups who preferred a quieter form of worship in which they sought God in a more direct way. Normally called Illuminists in Spain, they were often unjustly accused of Lutheranism. Another group, particularly strong in the universities, were admirers of the scholarship of Erasmus, whose liberal ideas, stressing the personal side of religion, proved unacceptable to Spanish authority. During the 1520s and 1530s therefore, the Inquisition took steps to extinguish both Illuminism and Erasmianism. In 1525 forty-eight Illuminist propositions were condemned, and the period 1529–33 saw trials and punishments of both groups to such an extent that, by the end of the 1530s, Illuminist societies had disappeared, the disciples of Erasmus had been expelled from the universities and many of his works prohibited.

This was a victory for the conservative forces who sought to insulate Spain from influences, whether from at home or abroad, which might undermine Spanish religion and society. Nor did their successes end with the triumph of orthodoxy in the 1530s. The Inquisition next turned its attention to the question of racial purity. During the 1540s this movement gathered force, and in 1547 Silecio, the Archbishop of Toledo, decreed that purity of blood was necessary to anyone holding church office in his diocese. This was soon extended to cover the whole of Castile, with the result that an air of suspicion was created, in which informers were employed to investigate irregularities in the lineage of rivals and enemies. Men were encouraged to condemn their neighbours in the secrecy of the Inquisition which, consequently, increased its power, and since few families were certain of being totally free from Jewish or Moorish blood the whole of society was affected.

This policy, although it proved to be detrimental to Spain in the long run, was wholeheartedly backed by Philip who, on the abdication of his father in 1556 confirmed the racial decrees, adding that 'all the heresies in Germany, France and Spain have been sown by descendants of the Jews'. Arriving in 1559 from the Netherlands, where he had seen heresy at first hand, Philip actively promoted the pursuit of orthodoxy and, in the search for uniformity, he permitted the provocation of the Morisco revolt and their subsequent expulsion from Granada between 1567 and 1570.

Fearing Calvinism above all, however, Philip gave strong backing to the Inquisitor General Valdes, who held the office from 1547 to 1566, and to his associate, the eminent Dominican Melchior Cano (d. 1560); in 1558 the importing of foreign books was forbidden and it was decreed that those printed in Spain needed to be licensed, while in the following year Spanish students were ordered not to travel or study abroad. The Index was revised and many books, including the *Enchiridion* of Erasmus, were listed which previously had been permitted. Meanwhile 'Protestant' communities had been discovered at Seville and Valladolid and, although they were little more than relics of Illuminist and Erasmian societies, the Inquisition determined to act.

Autos da fé were held and by the mid 1560s the problem was eradicated although at the expense of many executions. Nor was this the end. With Calvinism spreading in southern France Philip feared for the purity of the province of Catalonia. At the same time, therefore, as Alvà marched to extirpate heresy in the Netherlands, new and more stringent laws were made for the Catalans: in 1568 a harsh censorship was imposed, Frenchmen were forbidden to hold teaching posts in the province and a clearer prohibition was placed on Catalans studying abroad. In fact, Philip's fears proved groundless, both in Catalonia and in Spain as a whole, for neither Lutheranism nor Calvinism made much headway, although it may well be that this was due to prompt government action.

The 1560s were a frightening period for Roman Catholics throughout Europe, but this cannot excuse the inestimable harm done to Spanish society in the search for purity and for uniformity, for while Spain continued to exert a powerful influence on other countries, her own frontiers were closed to the influx of foreign ideas.

Philip, a devout Catholic, was dominated by the fear of heresy, believing that only the Crown could be trusted with the task of maintaining orthodoxy; furthermore, he was not prepared to allow any extension of papal power in Spain or her colonies, yet this threat faced all European nations after the Council of Trent. The Dominicans had long objected to the introduction of the Jesuits and Philip likewise feared them, although not as rivals, but as servants of the Papacy. Obstacles were therefore placed in their way and, compared with other orders, they were not especially numerous. Moreover, Philip did not confirm the decrees of Trent until 1565 and then only with the qualification that nothing should interefere with the Crown's right to influence ecclesiastical jurisdiction or to appoint bishops. Meanwhile Philip extended royal control over the Inquisition, and in the Italian colonies, especially Milan, his governors continued to object when Archbishop Borromeo and others sought to increase papal power. In 1572 having affirmed the Crown's right to scrutinise and, if necessary, to reject papal bulls before publication in Spain, Philip refused to accept a papal decree that Spaniards, when commanded to do so, should appear in foreign courts concerned with ecclesiastical cases. This arose out of the Carranza affair which symbolised the Crown's differences with the Papacy.

As Archbishop of Toledo and Primate of the Spanish Church Carranza had made many enemies, amongst them the Inquisitor General Valdes. Thus in 1559 he was arrested by the Inquisition and charged with heresy, but the debate on his beliefs was overshadowed by the bitter dispute which arose when Pius IV and Pius V demanded his removal to Rome for trial. Philip insisted that the Spanish Inquisition retained ultimate jurisdiction and, although Carranza was eventually moved to Rome in 1566, where he died ten years later, Philip had resisted long enough to win his point.

Thus for the first part of his reign Philip lived in a state of undeclared war with the Papacy, despite the necessity for concerted action against heresy. Nevertheless Spain remained the principal Catholic power in Europe and, during the 1570s, the Spanish Church reached new heights when, for a short period of time, a more liberal policy prevailed.

The defeat of heresy at home, the heroic defence of Malta in 1565 and the victory over the Turks at Lepanto in 1571, together with Alvà's active policy against the Dutch rebels, inspired a spirit of confidence throughout Castile. Cardinal Quiroga, appointed Inquisitor General in 1573 and Archbishop of Toledo in 1577, therefore felt able to pursue a more lenient policy in which the severity of the Inquisition was so relaxed that groups of scholars and mystics appeared, who deeply influenced the religious, intellectual and cultural life of the nation.

The greatest of these was undoubtedly St Teresa de Avila

(1515–82) whose life and work became an inspiration and an education to men and women throughout Europe. Well versed in the writings of earlier Spanish and foreign mystics such as Thomas à Kempis and Tauler, she explained the entry of the Holy Spirit into her soul, thus:

So I began to meditate on the place in hell which I deserved for my sins, and I gave great praises to God, for so changed was my life that I seemed not to recognise my own soul. While I was meditating in this way a strong impulse seized me without my realising it. It seemed as if my soul was about to leave the body, because it could no longer contain itself and was incapable of waiting for so great a blessing. The impulse was so exceedingly strong that it made me quite helpless. It was different, I think, from those which I had experienced on other occasions, and I did not know what was the matter with my soul, or what it wanted, so changed was it.

Strengthened by her new found convictions St Teresa determined to help others. Like many of her contemporaries she recognised that laxness of life within the orders was still a common fault; thus, accepting advice from Jesuits, Dominicans and Franciscans she founded, in 1562, the Discaled Carmelites at Avila who, by the time of her death twenty years later, possessed fourteen priories and sixteen convents. During the 1590s the total rose to eighty-one. In this venture St Teresa was particularly helped by her friend and disciple St John of the Cross (1542–91).

During the golden period of the 1570s even more orders pledged to stricter disciplines were established. Seventeen were set up in Madrid during Philip II's reign, together with other houses and hospitals, of which the most important were those attached to the Hospitaller Brothers of St John of God, officially recognised by Pius V in 1572. St John of God (1485–1550), a Portuguese, founded his first hospital in Granada in 1537, but it was only in the 1570s and 1580s that the order flourished, so much so that by 1590 it contained 600 brothers working in seventy-nine hospitals throughout the Spanish Empire. Meanwhile in 1582 Quiroga summoned the Twentieth Toledan Council with the object of bringing about an improve-

ment in the educational and living standards of the clergy, and
of enforcing the decrees of Trent more efficiently. These activities, above all, symbolised the renewed piety and vigour of the
Spanish Church which spread to almost every European
country by the seventeenth century.

Moreover, they were matched by the scholarly writings of the
period. Although St Teresa's were the best known she was by no
means alone for Quiroga helped to protect a group of humanist
scholars who attempted, with considerable success, to adapt the
humanist culture of the Renaissance to Spanish religion.
Montano, an important Hebrew scholar, worked on Biblical
texts but the most notable was Luis de Léon (1528–91) who,
from 1561 onwards, worked at the university of Salamanca,
where important developments in philosphy took place. In his
writings and in those of Mateo Aleman (1547–1609), although
man's sinful nature is stressed, so also is the availability of
redemption through man's good works and God's grace. Thus in
all fields of cultural and religious life, from the literature of Luis
de Léon and the paintings of El Greco to the charitable work of
St Teresa, optimism and a belief in the dignity of man is apparent.

The Council of Trent played only a minor role in creating this
outburst of religious energy. The main stimulus came from
within Spain itself, where political and military success and the
undoubted purity of the Church seemed to have overcome the
difficulties of the 1560s. This is illustrated by the part played by
the Jesuits. Despite opposition, colleges were founded at Valencia
in 1544, Valladolid, Barcelona and Gandia in 1545, Alcala in
1546, Salamanca in 1548 and Burgos in 1550, while the number
of Jesuits rose consistently, reaching an estimated 1,440 by 1580.
Consequently they established a firm hold on education which
gave them considerable power; nevertheless they neither
stimulated nor played such an important part in the revival in
Spain as they did elsewhere.

Unfortunately the vigour and the greater freedom in religious
life depended too much on the continued political and military
success of Spain and its Empire, a success which from the 1590s
was not maintained: the Armada, seen as a crusade against the

heretic, ended in disaster; failure in the Netherlands, economic crisis, plague and famine, and the degeneracy of the ruling family after 1598 shattered the illusion that Spain was specially favoured by God. Quarrels arose amongst the orders, particularly between Dominicans and Jesuits, and although the numbers of clergy remained high their quality did not; energy and creativeness were lost, excitement and curiosity died away, to be replaced in the seventeenth century by an atmosphere of fatalism and pessimism in which strict orthodoxy was re-enforced.

Spain was concerned also with the condition of the Church in the Netherlands, where attempts to enforce Castilian government and reformed Catholicism led to an eighty years' war. Philip stated that he would rather lose the Low Countries than continue to rule over them if they ceased to be Catholic; thus the Netherlands witnessed one of the earliest struggles between the forces of the Reformation and the Counter Reformation.

The Netherlands Church provided fertile ground for reforming ideas of all kinds. Lutheranism made considerable progress and Anabaptism was stronger than in any other part of Europe until Charles V's persecution checked the growth of both groups, but with the appearance of Calvinism in the southern provinces in the 1550s and 1560s the situation became critical. It was, therefore, principally against Calvinism that Philip directed the might of the Church, although, having left the Netherlands in 1559, despite the advice of Pius V and others, he never returned to give a personal lead.

During the 1550s the Inquisition, known as the 'Council of Blood', was introduced, closely followed in 1556 by the Jesuits who, despite only lukewarm support from the Crown, made a powerful impact, especially after the 1560s. In 1559 Philip introduced a scheme, prepared by his father, by which appointment to bishoprics would be brought more under royal control and their number increased from three to seventeen; Granvelle, Philip's chief minister, was to be Archbishop of Mechlin and Primate of the Netherlands Church.

Against this the nobility, fearing deprivation of their privileges, revolted and demanded the withdrawal of the Inquisition and all edicts against heresy. Philip, with the support of Pius V, responded by announcing in 1564 that the decrees of Trent would be enforced. In 1566 a popular revolt, centred around Calvinism in the southern provinces, broke out whereupon Philip determined to act more forcefully. By this time political and religious issues had become so inextricably linked that Philip equated Calvinism with rebellion, and on the eve of Alvà's departure for the Netherlands in 1567 he declared that

to negotiate with these people is so pernicious to God's service . . . that I have preferred to expose myself to the hazards of war . . . rather than allow the slightest derogation from the Catholic faith and the authority of the Holy See.

In the person of Alvà, the Counter Reformation appeared in its most militant form between 1567 and 1573. A policy of total repression based on the army and on a reconstituted Council of Blood was enforced, and by 1570 it seemed that the population had been frightened into submission. Revolt broke out anew, however, when the Sea Beggars, a militant group of Calvinists, having captured Brill in 1572, thence gained control of the principal towns of the maritime provinces of Holland and Zeeland where revolt proved much more difficult to quell.

Alvà was withdrawn in 1573 and under his successors Requesens (1573–6), Don John (1576–8) and Parma (1578–92) Philip proved willing to take a more conciliatory line on political questions but, significantly, not on religion. Indeed, in the crucial meeting at Breda in 1573 Requesens offered to respect Netherlands' privileges but stated that he was not empowered to make any religious concessions while, at a later date, Parma, although displaying supreme statesmanship in dealing with conquered provinces, refused to allow toleration.

In 1579 the Walloon provinces of the south, more accessible to Spanish power, tired of war and disliking William of Orange and the bourgeois oligarchies of the north, came to terms with the Spanish government in the Union of Arras, by which they accepted Roman Catholicism; as a result, the Church in those areas was gradually rebuilt. It remained, however, for the

Spanish to attempt the re-conquest of the northern provinces, formed in 1578 into the Union of Utrecht. Parma's army had such success that by 1587 it seemed that nothing could prevent the complete restoration of the Netherlands to Spain and to the Catholic Church, but by 1592 the tide had turned and Maurice of Nassau recovered many of Parma's conquests. Thereafter neither the northern provinces nor Spain was able to defeat the other, and the settlement made in the Truce of 1609 was based on the military boundary, which ensured that Flanders and southern Brabant, although racially and culturally tied to the north, remained in the Spanish Netherlands.

The consolidation of Catholicism in the south was the work of Archduke Albert, Governor between 1596 and 1621, from the Austrian branch of the Hapsburg family, and his Spanish wife Isabella. Their greatest advantage lay in the fact that during the wars opposition had either been silenced or expelled, thus society had become aristocratic and conservative; consequently their government was generally able to enforce its decisions. Both were devout Catholics who set an example by attending religious ceremonies, and so, after the Twelve Year Truce in 1609, strict regulations were laid down to strengthen the Catholic Church.

Although personal convictions were not too deeply enquired into and the harsh edicts of Philip II were never restored, outward conformity was demanded; priests were required to report on laxness amongst their congregations, and church attendance on Sundays was made compulsory; midwives were obliged to see that all children were baptised into the Catholic Church, and no one was allowed to teach or to preach without careful examination of their beliefs. Furthermore, strict censorship was imposed upon printers; the bishops acting as agents for the licensing of books and other publications. To ensure that the authority of the Church was upheld laymen were forbidden to discuss religious subjects; thus the imposition of Catholic orthodoxy did much to increase the conservatism of society in the Spanish Netherlands.

In enforcing these regulations Albert was assisted by the bishops, whom he appointed with care, by the Papal Nuncios and by the religious orders amongst whom there were many new foundations. Of these the most important were the groups of lay people who, joining together in the name of Mary to venerate the sacraments and to carry out works of charity, took their religion and piety into every aspect of daily life. None of the new societies, however, nor indeed any of the older ones could rival the power and influence of the Jesuits. Patronised by the government, although incurring deep suspicion from other orders, they were a vigorous force within the Church, particularly in education where the improvement in the quality of the priesthood was largely due to the instruction provided at Jesuit seminaries. Moreover their colleges for lay people, especially of the upper classes, ensured a constant flow of devout and obedient young men. The official catechism of the Church was written in 1607 by Father Makeblyde, a Jesuit, while the most important literary works in opposition to the heretics of the north were written by the Jesuit chief, Father Costerus, from Antwerp.

Albert's government, however, had little success in protecting or extending Roman Catholicism in the United Provinces where, although the majority remained Catholic, their influence diminished as they were gradually excluded, even in Gelderland and Overyssel where they had been most powerful, from positions of importance. The renewal of war in 1621 only increased these tendencies, although for a while the south kept up its attempts to keep the old religion alive. Jesuits were constantly to be found in the north, and in 1622 Rovenius was even consecrated Archbishop with responsibility for the United Provinces, later receiving the honorary title of Archbishop of Utrecht where, for a considerable period of time, he lived in hiding. Roman Catholicism was never extinguished in the United Provinces and, between 1600 and 1650 the number of communicants in Rotterdam may even have risen, but in reality the struggle was lost by 1609 and the Catholics of the north became passive and obscure.

Nevertheless, Catholicism was firmly re-established in the southern provinces – even in Flanders and southern Brabant. This success, however, was achieved at great cost for the Church,

supported by the government for political as well as for religious
reasons, clamped down on freedom of thought and stifled intellectual initiative. The provinces found their inspiration, as well
as their mode of government, in southern Europe – in Spain and
in Italy – and, although some fine examples of Baroque architecture were produced, as in the church of St Carlo Borromeo in
Brussels and, despite the paintings of Rubens (1577–1640), the
south could produce nothing to match the inventiveness and
culture of the United Provinces.

The forces of the Counter Reformation first appeared in England
during the reign of Mary Tudor (1553–8) who dedicated herself
to forming an alliance with Spain, and to revoking the religious
change introduced by her brother Edward VI and by her father
Henry VIII. Her marriage to Philip II proved universally
unpopular, as did England's entry into the war against France
which culminated in the loss of Calais in 1558, but in her
attempts to restore Roman Catholicism, initially she found
more support. Roman Catholics were released from prison, and
the Parliament of 1553 made little opposition to the repealing of
Edward VI's settlement, although making it clear that attempts
to interfere with ex-monastic land would be sternly resisted.

Mary was by no means satisfied with this, however, and after
Philip's arrival in 1554, despite his cautionary advice, she
plunged on, listening only to those who supported her policy. Using
her position as head of the Church which she denied in theory,
she removed unsuitable clergy, especially those who had married,
and returned church services to orthodox Catholicism. When, in
1554, Cardinal Pole returned from the continent to lend support,
the re-establishment of the Catholic Church was carried through
at even greater speed. Under pressure, the 1554 Parliament
repealed the reformation of Henry VIII and, to Mary's great
joy, Pole, on behalf of Paul IV, accepted England back into the
universal Church.

By this time, however, Mary's support had dwindled to the
few surviving papalists in England, yet still she determined to
press on. Parliament re-enacted the heresy laws which enabled

her and Pole to introduce persecution, unprecedented by English standards. Thus between 1555 and 1558, about 300 people, mostly poor and humble, but including the leading Protestants Cranmer, Ridley, Hooper and Latimer, were executed. In carrying through such a policy Mary placed herself outside the main stream of the Counter Reformation, for she acted entirely according to her own wishes and against the advice of Paul IV and of her husband, Philip. Her rule, which ensured that Elizabeth would have support for a Protestant settlement created a lasting fear of the link between Catholicism and the power of Spain.

Despite this, many devout Catholics remained in England after the settlement of 1559, and it was inevitable that the forces of the Counter Reformation would re-appear. As it turned out the crucial period proved to be Elizabeth's reign itself, and although the attempt came too late to succeed, Roman Catholicism was preserved as a minority religion; it is, however, arguable that this could have been achieved if Catholics had taken no action whatever, but simply conformed outwardly to the Anglican Church.

Fifteen of the sixteen bishops still in office in 1559 refused to take the oath of Supremacy to Elizabeth, retiring instead into private life where they caused the government little concern. No other personalities, inside or outside Parliament, at home or abroad, arose to inspire English Catholics who remained leaderless throughout the 1560s; indeed, Philip II, later to lead the attack on Elizabeth, protected her during this period, through fear of France, and without his assistance the Papacy could achieve little. Consequently, in the formative years of the Church of England, the Counter Reformation failed to organise its forces and the main opportunity was lost. Thereafter the chances of success were extremely limited.

It is impossible to estimate accurately the number of practising Catholics in England after 1559, but there were undoubtedly a great many, particularly in the extreme north, in Cheshire, in Lancashire, where the Stanley family protected them, in the west country and even in London where they congregated in the

Spanish Embassy chapel. Only about 300 out of 8,000 priests refused the oath of Supremacy, although others certainly continued to conduct traditional services, if not in the parish church, then in the houses of sympathetic local gentry. The government had no wish, at this stage, to pry into men's consciences, therefore, despite the papal decree of 1563 that English Catholics should not attend Anglican churches, the majority clearly did so, those choosing to stay away presumably being willing to pay the, not excessive, recusancy fine of one shilling per Sunday for non attendance.

Catholicism certainly survived the initial years of Elizabeth's reign, although in a passive and unobtrusive way; perhaps when it was seen that Elizabeth did not intend to make windows into men's souls the numbers even increased, for in 1570 the Bishop of Carlisle declared that in Lancashire

On all hands the people fall from religion, revolt to Popery, refuse to come to Church; the wicked papist priests reconcile them to the Church of Rome and cause them to abjure their religion; and that openly and unchecked.

The bishop was probably exaggerating, for it is very doubtful whether Catholicism, severed from its roots abroad, could have survived the passage of time and the generations. Nevertheless it remained alive and, indeed, its character suited many Catholic gentry who, employing a Catholic priest within their household did, like Lord Vaux in 1581, 'claim his house to be a parish by itself'. In this way they exerted control over the priest and over religious matters to a greater extent than ever before.

Inevitably this situation was disturbed by more ardent spirits who, not satisfied with the mere survival of Catholicism, wished to overthrow the Anglican Church. These men, inspired by and in touch with the leaders of the European Counter Reformation, were to be found mostly amongst English Catholics who had accepted voluntary exile rather than live under Elizabeth's settlement. Not all the exiles, however, were thus inclined, indeed the earliest groups, including some of the finest minds from Oxford and Cambridge, settled in the southern

Netherlands at Louvain, where they meditated and wrote on the state of the Church in general and of English Catholicism in particular, awaiting the day when reason and good sense would prevail and England would revert to the true religion.

Some, however, decided that such passive waiting was a forlorn hope. Foremost amongst these was the ex-Oxford don and future cardinal William Allen (1532–94), who did more than any other man to lead the attempt at reconversion. Having visited England after Elizabeth's settlement, but failing to persuade English Catholics of their duty to stay away from the Anglican parish churches, he determined to initiate a more active policy and, to this end, he moved from Louvain to Douai where in 1568, he founded a college to train English priests. Like Louvain, Douai produced pamphlets and literature defending English Catholicism and in the ensuing paper war the translation in 1582 of the Vulgate Bible into English by the ex-Oxford don Gregory Martin was probably the most important single contribution. Moreover, even when, between 1578 and 1593, the college was forced to move to Rheims its influence remained powerful.

Nevertheless, Allen, realising that much of the opposition to the Catholic Church had been caused by its own shortcomings, insisted that the Douai priests should be carefully trained and educated, particularly in the details of pastoral care. Thus a devout and energetic breed of men were produced and between 1574 and 1603 the college sent 438 priests to England, the first of whom Louis Barlow, Henry Shaw, Martin Nelson and Thomas Meetham, landed in 1574. Many were to die for their faith but all strengthened the resolve of those people with whom they came into contact.

In 1577 Cuthbert Mayne, having landed in Cornwall was captured near Truro and executed at Launceston Castle; the first martyr from Douai, his crime was that he infringed the 1571 statute which forbad anyone to introduce, or to attempt to implement, the Papal Bull of Excommunication. The bull, part of a separate attempt to reconvert England, led by the Papacy, linked with Spain and supported by aggressive exiles such as

Nicholas Parsons and Allen himself, ironically laid a serious handicap on the work of the Douai priests.

The 1570 Bull of Excommunication was the impetuous action of Pius V, based on the advice of certain exiles, particularly Nicholas Sanders and Nicholas Morton, who assured him that English Catholics were ready to rebel. Their evidence was based largely on knowledge of the Northern Rebellion of 1569, when Catholic noblemen, encouraged by Spain and the Papacy, raised a semi-feudal revolt against the lengthening arm of central government. For this revolt, however, there was little general support and when, early in the morning of 15 May 1570, John Felton nailed the bull to the door of the Bishop of London's palace the Northern Rising, unbeknown to the Papacy, had already been crushed. The bull itself was neither carefully worded nor clearly thought out but, above all, it placed English Catholics, priests and laymen in the dilemma of choosing between religion and country:

We do out of the fullness of our apostolic power declare the aforesaid Elizabeth to be a heretic . . . and moreover we declare her to be deprived of her pretended title to the aforesaid crown. We charge and command all and singular the nobles, subjects, people and others aforesaid that they do not dare obey her orders, mandates and laws. Those who shall act to the contrary we include in the like sentence of excommunication.

Faced with this choice the majority maintained a loyalty to the Queen, which they confirmed in the critical days of the Armada, eighteen years later. Nevertheless the government was forced to re-assess its position and when the Douai priests and other missionaries landed, they were treated as papal and Spanish agents. This attitude was increased by further developments. In 1577 Mary, Queen of Scots, having disinherited her son James, turned to Spain for help in obtaining the English throne. The plots which followed – Throckmorton's in 1583 and Babington's in 1586 – together with fear of the growth of Spain's power induced Elizabeth to act, but by sending Leicester to help the Dutch rebels in 1585 and by executing Mary in 1587, she incited Philip into launching the Armada.

Meanwhile in the 1570s the Papacy, supported by Spanish troops, made two attempts to attack Elizabeth through Ireland. In 1578 Gregory XIII, encouraged by the visit to Rome of the Irish rebel James Fitzmaurice Fitzgerald, despatched an expedition under the command of an Englishman, Sir Thomas Stukeley, which came to nothing since, under the persuasion of the King of Portugal, Stukeley diverted his forces to Morocco where he was defeated. A year later, however, Fitzgerald, aided by Nicholas Sanders as legate and backed by Spanish troops, landed in southern Ireland but despite initial success the expedition failed miserably. The English deputy in Ireland, Grey de Wilton, defeated the Spanish troops in 1580, Fitzgerald was killed in 1579 and Nicholas Sanders died in 1581. Twenty years later, in 1601, Spain gave similar support, in the form of 3,000 troops, to the equally ill-fated rebellion of Tyrone.

The aims of the Papacy and the attempt to restore Catholicism thus became dependent upon the military power of Spain; hence the Catholic gentry gave virtually no support to the movement, while the English government was driven to enact harsher measures. These developments were increased by the advent in 1580 of the Jesuits. After founding the college at Douai, Allen sought their support and in 1579 a Jesuit Seminary for the training of English missionaries was founded in Rome. The first Jesuits to reach England, in 1580, were two ex-Oxford dons, Edmund Campion and Nicholas Parsons, supported by a Jesuit lay brother. At their request, before they left Rome Gregory XIII had defined their position with regard to the execution of the 1570 Bull of Excommunication. Since Gregory recognised that, for the moment, the bull could not be enforced, he decreed that Campion and Parsons should not be bound by it, and that they should not challenge the loyalty of Englishmen to Elizabeth. Campion declared in England that

My charge is to preach the gospel, to minister the sacraments, to instruct the simple, to reform sinners, to confute errors, and, in brief, to cry alarm spiritual against foul vice and proud ignorance wherewith my dear countrymen are abused. I never had mind and am

strictly forbidden by our fathers that sent me, to deal in any respect
with matters of state or policy of the realm as those things which
appertain not to my vocation.

Despite this the government found the overall situation, at
home and abroad, too serious to risk leniency and when, in 1581,
the gentle and saintly Campion was captured he was executed.
Parsons, who escaped in 1581 and who lived until 1610, was with
Allen the great organiser of the missions to England; he fully
supported the Spanish Armada, in 1589 he set up a college for
English priests at Valladolid and another shortly afterwards at
Seville, while he constantly helped to keep open the routes
through Spain, France and the Low Countries by which the
missionaries reached England. The Jesuits continued to operate
in England, producing such influential figures as Father Garnet,
who led them from 1586 to 1605, Robert Southwell and John
Gerard and it was rumoured that as late as 1625 there were 125
still present in the country although, as elsewhere in Europe,
they exerted an influence far beyond their numbers.

The government maintained its repressive policy, and by the
end of the reign approximately 250 men had been executed, of
whom about half were priests trained abroad. This persecution
did much to prevent the success of the Counter Reformation
but many other factors played their part: the Catholic gentry
never gave their full support for, although many protected the
priests, they came to resent the fact that they were forced into
choosing between religion and country or that they might once
more have to accept the authority of priests. These feelings were
intensified when it was seen that Allen, Parsons and others were
actively supporting Spanish military activities, thus the exiles
became extremely unpopular.

Furthermore the exiles themselves were bitterly divided. Many
of those taken prisoner were kept in Wisbech castle where,
during the 1590s, arguments arose which became public; in
particular, the ordinary priests resented the activities of the
Jesuits who, it seemed, were trying to control the whole movement and who received more praise then their efforts deserved.

Thus by the death of Elizabeth the attempt against England had failed and, racked by internal dissensions, English Catholicism seemed a spent force. Whether the Elizabethan martyrs died in vain is an open question, although it is probable that even without their sacrifice Catholicism would have survived. Above all, however, they were inadequately led, for the forces of the Counter Reformation against England were never coherently or consistently organised.

Nevertheless, hopes were raised at the accession of James I of a more tolerant attitude and, despite his pronouncements to the contrary, the laws against Catholics were not as vigorously enforced. A brief revival of Catholicism ensued which, together with fear engendered by the Bye and Main plots of 1603–4 involving several priests, frightened James into a more thorough enforcement of the penal laws. This provoked the ill fated Gunpowder Plot which, permanently associating Catholicism with treason, might well have led to the extinction of English Catholicism. In fact it failed to do so, and thereafter persecution varied in intensity largely according to the government's foreign policy.

During the 1630s a revival, led by Henrietta Maria, wife to Charles I, took place at the court itself but there was no chance of a large scale conversion, and Roman Catholics remained in English society as a passive and, generally, loyal element denying links with the political Counter Reformation on the continent. The final proof appeared in the reign of James II (1685–8) when all attempts at re-conversion met unassailable opposition.

During the reign of Elizabeth and throughout the seventeenth century, Ireland successfully resisted all English attempts at conversion; the Elizabethan conquest was followed by the Cromwellian settlements but to no avail. Ireland endured as a centre of the Roman Catholic Church whose priests remained a powerful influence in society. On the other hand the forces of the Counter Reformation failed entirely to make any impression on Scotland. The removal of French influence in 1560 and the defeat of Mary, Queen of Scots, in 1586 ensured the success of Knox's

Protestant movement. Nevertheless, in 1579, Esme Stuart, backed by the Guise in France, worked his way into the favour of James VI, with the intention of restoring both French and Catholic influence; his downfall in 1583, however, served not only to destroy the French movement but also any further efforts at Counter Reformation.

Although there was little Protestantism in Portugal, a great deal was done to ensure the purity of the Church. John III (1521–57), a devout Catholic, asked the pope in 1531 to grant Portugal a permanent Inquisition and when, in 1539–40, he learned of the work of the Jesuits in Italy he requested their assistance also. Despite this the progress of reform did not run smoothly for to both moves there was opposition. John insisted, however, and the Inquisition was established in 1536 while the Jesuits, led by Rodrigues de Azevedo, who obtained great influence over the King, soon secured a permanent and powerful position.

Rodrigues was appointed tutor to John's son and another Jesuit became confessor to Henry, the King's brother, who had initially opposed the invitation to the Jesuits. A Jesuit College was founded at Coimbra and later, in 1547, when the government established a new college there, this also was handed over to the Jesuits. So influential did they become, in fact, that John refused to allow the pope to recall Rodrigues, even when it seemed that the Portuguese Jesuits were virtually setting up an independent society. Disputes also arose when Henry, as Inquisitor General, attempting to enforce absolute orthodoxy, aroused such opposition that the pope was forced to step in and suspend the Inquisition. Although a compromise was reached in 1548 by which Henry was made a Cardinal and the Inquisition re-opened, arguments continued and the Papacy was never satisfied that its wishes were being followed.

Portugal's greatest contribution to the Counter Reformation was undoubtedly the missionary work carried on in her overseas empire. When John requested the presence of Jesuits in 1539 it was mainly for this purpose; thus Francis Xavier, the greatest of all overseas missionaries of the period, arrived in Portugal in 1540, to embark two years later on a lifetime's work in the Far East (see page 156).

Largely because of their proximity to Italy and thanks to the support of the Duke of Savoy several Swiss cantons returned to the Catholic faith towards the end of the sixteenth century. Borromeo was able to exert pressure, and students poured into the cantons from his college at Milan, at the same time as the Jesuits and Capucins established themselves. In 1586 the five forest cantons of Uri, Schwyz, Unterwalden, Lucerne and Zug joined with Soleure and Freibourg in a pact, organised by Borromeo, by which they agreed to maintain and defend Roman Catholicism. These designs were assisted by the work of St Francis de Sales (see page 154) who, accepting the honorary title of Bishop of Geneva in 1602, and patronised by the Duke of Savoy, promoted the Catholic faith in Chablais.

[17]   THE STRUGGLE FOR CENTRAL EUROPE

In the half century after Luther's protest the situation in Germany grew progressively worse for the Catholic Church, not merely in the sense that Lutheranism gained ground but in that the Church proved unable to reform itself or to cope with the Protestant attack. In 1540 Eck wrote 'I know one cathedral church where only three out of fifty-four canons are priests', while elsewhere it was noted that the interest of the canons was about evenly divided between horses, dogs and women. Moreover, in the later 1540s neither the university of Cologne nor Ingolstadt possessed a Professor of Theology and when Emperor Ferdinand I searched for suitable theologians to send to the third Session of the Council of Trent he was unable to find any.

On the other hand, the Lutherans and, particularly after mid-century, the Calvinists continued to make great progress, and no area of Germany remained unaffected; to such an extent that in 1557 the Venetian ambassador reported that nine-tenths of Germany had become Protestant. Even the predominantly Catholic north-west and south-east were affected. Faced with such a situation the Catholic princes, including Emperors Ferdinand I (1556–64) and Maximilian II (1564–76), were compelled to grant concessions, so much so that the Papacy quarrelled bitterly with Ferdinand, while for a time there was a danger that Maximilian might even turn Protestant himself.

The most significant concession was the Peace of Augsburg of 1555, by which Ferdinand recognised the right of the German princes to choose either Catholicism or Lutheranism as their state religion. The settlement, however, created as many problems as it solved, since rival interpretations produced quarrels for the next half a century; nevertheless, two clauses were especially relevant to the later revival of the Catholic Church. Ferdinand declared that in the free cities a parity should be maintained between the two faiths which, at least from a legal standpoint, preserved Catholicism in the urban centres. More important, however, was the ecclesiastical reservation clause which Ferdinand also insisted upon.

And since it has proved to be matter of great dispute what was to happen with the bishoprics, priories, and other ecclesiastical benefices of such Catholic priests as would in course of time abandon the old religion, we have in virtue of the powers of Roman Emperors ordained as follows: Where an archbishop, bishop or prelate or any other priest of our old religion shall abandon the same, his archbishopric, bishopric, prelacy, and other benefices, together with all their income and revenues which he has so far possessed, shall be abandoned by him without any further objection or delay.

Although Protestants argued that when a man was converted to Protestantism before receiving a benefice then he could retain it, together with its benefits, the ecclesiastical reservation clause did more than any other legal act to ensure the preservation of powerful and wealthy benefices for the Catholic Church. Despite this the situation remained gloomy until well into the 1570s and 1580s by which time it seemed that nothing could prevent the complete loss of Germany. It so happened, however, that the

Protestants became increasingly divided. After Luther's death in 1546 the Lutherans quarrelled amongst themselves, while, from the 1560s, the advent of Calvinism further complicated the issue, particularly when in the reign of Elector Frederick III (1559–76), the Palatinate became Calvinist, followed shortly by Nassau. It was therefore the greatest good fortune for Catholicism that these divisions coincided with a revival within the Roman Catholic Church itself. The revival, which appeared between the 1560s and 1580s, centred principally on a number of devout groups, particularly in the Rhineland, and on several secular princes, including Emperor Rudolph II (1576–1612) and Albert V (1550–79) of Bavaria. From the beginning, foreign influences, especially Spanish and Italian, played a vital role in the recovery, yet their importance should not obscure the lead given by Germans themselves who were always deeply involved in the movement.

Although the Jesuits settled in Cologne, at the invitation of local groups, in 1544 it was not until the 1560s, when their colleges and universities began to produce suitable young men, that they made much progress Ferdinand I allowed them into the University of Vienna in 1551 and this was followed by their entry into the universities of Prague in 1556, Munich in 1559, Trier in 1560, Innsbruck in 1561, and Braunsberg, Dillingen, Speyer and Würzburg during the 1560s; moreover, by 1578, they had complete control of the arts and theological faculties of Cologne. Loyola founded a college in Rome in 1552 for the training of German priests, but this failed through internal dissension, and it was not until Gregory XIII reconstituted it in 1573 that its useful life began. By 1580, therefore, Jesuit influence had made a profound impact throughout Germany.

This was achieved not only by their work at the colleges and universities, for by their preaching and by their charitable works they restored to the common people of Germany a faith in the vigour and purity of the Church. In this, the greatest single contribution was made by Peter Canisius (1521–97). Converted to the Jesuits while at Cologne, Canisius became firstly a preacher and missionary then a teacher, confessor and organiser. As preacher and missionary he displayed a marvellous ability to explain the fundamentals of the Catholic faith to people of all classes, the catechism which he produced after 1555 running into hundreds of editions; as teacher and organiser he passed successively through the universities of Cologne, Ingolstadt and Vienna, and between 1556 and 1569 he was the official director of the Upper German Provinces of the Jesuit Order, which included Switzerland, Swabia, Bavaria and the hereditary Hapsburg lands. During his stay in Vienna he acted as confessor to the Hapsburg court, where his influence over Rudolph I was of crucial importance in obtaining imperial support for the Counter Reformation.

Although often indecisive and, later in life, withdrawn and probably insane, Rudolph II (1576–1612) was a devout Catholic who had been educated in Spain, partially by the Jesuits. Thus at an early stage of the revival of the Church in Germany, he was able to provide imperial support in a number of important incidents. Nevertheless, the most active secular princes were the Wittelsbachs in Bavaria, where reform was initiated by Albert V (1550–79).

Albert's fight against his Lutheran nobility was political as much as religious but, with papal assistance, the opposition was overcome. In 1570 a Spiritual Council was established which, by diocesan visitations, by a strict supervision of education and by the introduction and enforcement of the Trent decrees gradually reformed the Bavarian Church. A censorship, based largely on an Index drawn up by Canisius, was begun in 1569 and the Jesuits, entering Munich university in 1559, Dillingen in 1563 and by 1576 dominating Ingolstadt, achieved almost complete control of education, particularly of the upper and middle classes. Moreover, in 1578 they founded an entirely new college at Landshut. Under William V (1579–97) and Maximilian I (1597–1651), who was himself educated by the Jesuits at Ingolstadt, the policy grew harsher as the government sought to establish political absolutism together with religious orthodoxy. Protestants were forced to leave, church attendance became compulsory and attempts were made to enforce Catholic faith and morality both in public and in private. The reform of the Bavarian Church which became the backbone of the recovery in Germany inevitably affected neighbouring areas, for the ambitions of the Wittelsbachs knew no bounds.

In extending their political power the Wittelsbachs also re-established Catholicism in Freising, where the twelve year old Prince Ernest was appointed bishop in 1566, and in Regensburg, where the three year old Prince Philip obtained a similar position in 1579. Furthermore, in 1607-8, the free city of Donauworth was brought under Bavarian rule after Maximilian, acting on the Emperor's behalf, had entered the city, ejected the Protestant majority from its council and restored it to Catholicism. Meanwhile Wolff Dietrich von Raittenau, Archbishop of neighbouring Salzburg (1587-1612), despite living the life of a typical German prince, complete with concubine and offspring, returned his diocese firmly to the Catholic faith. In all these actions the government's primary consideration was to increase its political power – although Maximilian was undoubtedly a devout Catholic – hence Bavarian influence was soon felt in other parts of Germany, particularly in the north-west.

Meeting his first diet in 1582 at Augsburg, Rudolph II faced, and successfully dealt with, a crisis which helped to decide the future of north-western Germany. Prince Joachim Frederick, a Lutheran, attended the diet as Archbishop of Magdeburg, a position which, according to the ecclesiastical reservation clause of 1555, he was not entitled to hold. The Catholics objected, Rudolph upheld their protests and Prince Joachim withdrew, thus clearly establishing the precedent to be applied in the crucial dispute which arose in Cologne between 1582 and 1585. The Archbishop of Cologne, Gebhard Truchsess von Waldburg, after much thought and discussion, announced in 1582 his conversion to Protestantism and his marriage, declining thereafter to renounce his benefices, his titles or his incomes, and declaring freedom of worship for Protestants within the diocese. The Papacy formally deposed Gebhard, but it was Bavarian military strength which proved decisive, since only John Casimir, with Palatinate troops, moved to defend him.

In return for Bavaria's assistance Prince Ernest, already Bishop of Freising, of Hildesheim and of Liège, was elected Archbishop of Cologne in 1585. Although a pluralist and an unsuitable character, Ernest brought with him the might of Bavaria and the vigour of its Church, but above all, the ecclesiastical reservation clause was upheld and the archbishop's electoral vote remained in Catholic hands. Furthermore the success in Cologne acted as an encouragement for further progress.

In Trier, Archbishop Jacob von Eltz (1567–81) had already taken a strong line, bringing in the Jesuits in 1570, enforcing the decrees of Trent, excluding Protestants from office and improving the standards of his clergy by regular visitations; policies which were continued by his successors, notably by Lothair von Metternich (1559–1623). The same was true of Mainz, where the Jesuits were also introduced, and where Archbishops Adam von Bicken (1601–4), who had been educated at the Jesuit college in Rome, and Schweikard von Kronenberg (1604–20) completely eliminated Protestantism. In 1585 Prince Ernest of Bavaria added to his other titles the bishopric of Munster where he enforced the Catholic faith. In the neighbouring sees of Osnabruck and Paderborn the Church also recovered its vigour and removed heresy, Theodore von Furstenberg (1585–1618) introducing the Jesuits into Paderborn and after 1596 imprisoning priests who administered communion in both kinds, while from 1585 onwards Bernard von Waldeck insisted on a strict orthodoxy in Osnabruck. Meanwhile, in the important duchy of Cleves Julich, Duke William (1592–1609), a zealous Catholic, invited in the Jesuits and did much to restore the Catholic faith.

Central Germany saw a similar revival of the Roman Church in the same period, this time centred on the abbey of Fulda and the bishoprics of Würzburg and Bamberg. When Balthasar von Dembach became Abbot of Fulda in 1570 he broke a line of six Protestant abbots, thereby accepting the difficult task of attempting to restore the abbey lands to Catholicism. His life was spent in bitter struggle – between 1576 and 1596 he was even forced by the nobility and powerful middle classes to leave his charge – but ultimately, helped by the Papacy and the Jesuits, the area was reconverted. Julius Echter von Mespelbronn Bishop of Würzburg from 1573 to 1619 was, temporarily, a Protestant who opposed Balthazar in Fulda but, seeing the weakness of the Protestants and beginning to take his duties more seriously, he accepted the Catholic faith, ultimately becoming the finest example of a Counter Reformation prince-bishop in Germany. Helped by the Jesuits, whose college at Würzburg was elevated into a university in 1582, he made visitations throughout the diocese with such success that, by 1586, it was said that fourteen towns, including Würzburg itself in 1587, two hundred villages and in all 62,000 souls had been recovered. In addition, many churches were built or rebuilt and an air of vitality produced. In neighbouring Bamberg Archbishops Ernest von Mengersdorf (1583–91) and Neidhardt von Thurgen (1591–8) emulated the work done in Würzburg, insisting and actually enforcing that the population should either accept the mass or leave the area.

Thus by the early years of the seventeenth century Catholicism, largely because of its appeal to princes who strove to increase or confirm their political authority, (see page 166) had regained considerable ground in north-west, central and southern Germany although as yet no progress had been made in the north-eastern areas dominated by Saxony and Brandenburg. The characters of many of the prince-bishops left much to be desired yet, as in the case of Prince Ernest of Bavaria, they still enforced Catholicism on their subjects; in this they were greatly assisted by the papal nuncios, an increasing number of whom were appointed to Germany in the latter part of the century, Vienna, Munich and Cologne becoming permanent seats. By helping in the enforcement of the Trent decrees, they also ensured that papal policy was followed while their advice was invaluable, one of their number, Bonomi, urging in 1585 that 'the best way to fight the heretics is not to deserve their criticisms'.

Nonetheless Bavaria had given the lead and in 1609, as a reaction to the forming of the Protestant Evangelical Union by Frederick of the Palatinate, Maximilian founded the Roman

Catholic League for the defence of Catholicism, consisting of southern and north-western Catholic states patronised by Spain, but not connected with the Emperor. The League had many weaknesses and in 1617 Maximilian reconstituted it to include only south German princes, but it clearly illustrated the polarization of religious views which, from the Cleves Julich dispute in 1609 to the Treaty of Westphalia in 1648, was partly the cause of a series of wars which involved most German states and which ultimately settled Germany's religious boundaries.

During the Thirty Years' War (1618–48), Maximilian and the new Emperor, Ferdinand II (1619–37) of Styria attempted to strengthen their political authority and to extend Catholicism, at first in alliance, but after 1625 usually at odds with one another. From 1620 onwards, Spanish and Bavarian troops overran the Palatinate and removed its Elector, Frederick. Military conquest was followed by a reconversion, in which the Jesuits were introduced. This was partially successful, for, by the Treaty of Westphalia of 1648, Maximilian retained the Upper Palatinate, bordering his Bavarian territories which consequently permanently embraced the Catholic faith.

In the latter years of the 1620s, Emperor Ferdinand, backed by the military strength of Wallenstein, sought to re-establish Catholicism in north Germany between the Weser and the Oder where Protestantism was strongest. For a while no one seemed capable of standing in his way and by the Edict of Restitution of 1629 he decreed that the land settlement decided upon at Augsburg in 1555 would be enforced. This would have affected two archbishoprics, twelve bishoprics and many other important areas, and Ferdinand immediately appointed Hapsburgs and Wittelsbachs to sees at Bremen, Verden, Halberstadt and elsewhere. Some areas, such as Würtemberg in the south and Brunswick in the north were quickly affected, but over a wider area the edict proved unenforceable. The opposition to any increase in imperial power of both Catholic and Protestant princes, including Maximilian, the advent of Gustavus Adolphus of Sweden in 1630 and the loss of Wallenstein ensured that Ferdinand would not be able to carry out his plans for Germany.

By the Peace of Prague in 1635 the Emperor revoked the Edict of Restitution, thereby permanently restoring bishoprics such as Bremen, Verden and Halberstadt to Lutherans; moreover, the continued presence of Sweden ensured that there would be no further Catholic revival in north Germany. During the 1630s and 1640s religion became even less of an issue in the wars, although the Peace of Westphalia contained important religious clauses; Calvinism was officially recognised in the Empire but the Catholics lost none of their earlier gains, except the lower Palatinate. As at Augsburg in 1555, the prince was given the right to choose his religion but he was no longer permitted to enforce his faith on his subjects. The period of the Thirty Years' War, therefore, did little to help Catholicism in Germany itself. The work carried out by the Wittelsbachs of Bavaria, by the religious orders, notably the Jesuits, by the papal nuncios and with the support of the Emperor at the end of the sixteenth and the beginning of the seventeenth century, was decisive. This was recognised in the religious boundaries and agreed upon at Westphalia.

Even more striking than the achievements in Germany was the success of the Counter Reformation in the Hapsburg lands of south-east Europe, where Austria, Bohemia, Moravia, Silesia and Hungary had been deeply affected by Protestant views. Moreover in times of weakness, successive emperors had been forced to grant political and religious concessions. In 1571 Maximilian permitted Lutheran worship in Upper and Lower Austria and shortly afterwards even greater concessions were accorded to Styria and Carinthia. In Bohemia, Protestantism became linked with Hussite beliefs, while in Moravia the Anabaptists, known as the Moravian Brethren, gained a firm foothold. Despite this the latter years of the sixteenth century saw the Hapsburg rulers, encouraged and supported by Philip II through the Spanish Ambassador Guillen de San Clemente, take an effective stand against the further growth of heresy.

In the Tyrol Protestantism made little progress and Roman Catholicism remained dominant. This was by not so, however, in

CENTRAL EUROPE, *showing places referred to in the text*

Inner Austria (consisting of Styria, Carinthia and Carniola) where the government was in the hands, first of Archduke Charles (1564–90), and then of his son Ferdinand (1595–1637), later to be Emperor. Despite being compelled to grant concessions in the 1570s, Charles struggled effectively against the twin forces of political and religious opposition. Gregory XIII sent money and a papal nuncio; Albert of Bavaria, helped with advice and by example and, when the Jesuits were introduced a university was founded in 1586 at Graz under their direction. In the meantime Charles, attempting to divide the opposition, ensured that no Protestants were employed at the court or in government and, after 1582, they were gradually deprived of their rights.

The death of Charles allowed a brief reaction in favour of Protestantism, but Ferdinand, educated by the Jesuits at Ingolstadt, determined to carry on his father's work asserting that 'I would rather rule a country ruined than a country damned'. In fact under his strict paternalistic rule Inner Austria was neither ruined nor damned. In 1597 he made a personal vow to Clement VIII to restore the true faith and in the following year Protestant preachers were banished under pain of death, their churches closed and citizens were forced to accept Catholicism or renounce their civic rights, In the face of such a harsh policy large numbers chose to emigrate, perhaps as many as 10,000; but, by the early years of the seventeenth century, Catholicism was restored, at least outwardly, although there is no doubt that many of the nobility remained Lutheran.

After 1576 Rudolph II attempted to impose a similar restoration of the faith on Upper and Lower Austria, that area centred on the Danube and upstream from Vienna; in this, Melchior Khesl, Bishop of Vienna in 1598 and later a cardinal, was the prime agent. Protestants were excluded from the government and Rudolph, having forbidden Protestant worship in Vienna, expelled Lutheran preachers from Lower Austria between 1578 and 1580. In addition Canisius's catechism was introduced together with a strict censorship of all publications. This treatment was extended to Upper Austria after about 1600, and in both areas the government's hand was strengthened by a serious peasant rising in 1598 which the nobility helped suppress, thereby losing the support of the lower ranks of society. Thus, as in Germany, the restoration of the Catholic faith was part of the process by which the Government established absolute authority and, although much remained to be done, by the early seventeenth century the Hapsburgs had laid a firm foundation in Austria. This was not the case, however, in the associated territories of Bohemia, Moravia, Silesia and Lusatia.

The Counter Reformation, largely in the hands of the Hapsburg rulers and the Jesuit order, appeared in these areas early in the seventeenth century but with little success, even in Bohemia where efforts were concentrated against the Bohemian Brethren. Nevertheless some success might have followed but for the confusion into which the Hapsburg family fell after 1600. When Emperor Rudolph became ill his authority was challenged by his brother Matthais. Although a compromise was patched up in 1608 the family's weakness, accentuated by a renewed Turkish threat on the Danube, was clearly shown in new concessions given to the Lutherans of Upper and Lower Austria and in the Letters of Majesty, which granted a considerable degree of political and religious independence to Bohemia in 1609. Even when Matthias became Emperor in 1612 the situation was not improved, for by that time religious tensions in Germany were rising to a crisis.

It was not until the Hapsburgs selected Ferdinand of Styria to succeed to the imperial title that the progress, made around the turn of the century, could be continued. In 1617 Ferdinand became King of Bohemia, in 1618 King of Hungary and in 1619, on the death of Matthias, Holy Roman Emperor. From his accession in 1617 Ferdinand made clear his intention of reenforcing Catholicism in Bohemia; hence the Protestants, supported also by those who feared the loss of political independence, demanded the confirmation of the Letters of Majesty, and after the defenestration of Prague in 1618 the country flared into revolt. The Bohemians failed to obtain the full cooperation of Moravia, Lusatia and Silesia and, since religious, political and racial issues were hopelessly intermingled, no basic unity could be achieved; nevertheless the rebellion provided Ferdinand with the opportunity to act. Combining imperial troops with those of Maximilian of Bavaria under Tilly, he crushed the rebels at the battle of the White Mountain in 1620, thereafter Bohemia, isolated from foreign help, was at the Emperor's mercy.

In 1620 confiscation of Protestant lands began. Twenty-six leading nobles were executed, their estates being given to loyal Catholics, thereby creating a class dependent upon the Hapsburg family and upon the Catholic Church. Protestant preachers were expelled, their churches closed down and in the years following the victory at the White Mountain perhaps as many as 150,000 people emigrated from Bohemia and Moravia, thus eliminating the hard core of political and religious opposition. In 1627 Bohemia and Moravia were deprived of any semblance of political independence, both becoming hereditary domains of the Hapsburg emperors. By this time also, Protestantism had been extinguished and Catholicism fully re-enforced.

The military victories of the 1620s enabled Ferdinand to extend these policies throughout Austria. By 1628, 900 members of the nobility of Styria and Carinthia had left and thousands of other Austrians went into voluntary exile, thus removing those who might have led opposition to church or state. This allowed the consolidation of Catholicism to go forward, largely in the hands of the Jesuits who, by 1675, possessed six universities, fifty-five colleges and twenty-eight seminaries within the Hapsburg territories, thereby gaining almost complete control of education. The only Hapsburg lands not re-converted were Silesia and Lusatia, which, in return for John George of Saxony's non-intervention, were left alone, eventually passing into Saxon hands.

Ferdinand's success in south-east Europe included considerable achievements in the frontier lands of Hungary, at that time partially controlled by the Turks and partially by the Hapsburgs. Hungary had been greatly influenced by Swiss reformers, Calvinism, in particular, gaining ground after the middle years of the sixteenth century, usually associating itself with political opposition to Hapsburg rule. The reaction against this process began under Rudolph II and Nicholas Olahus, Archbishop of Gran until 1568. Olahus, having introduced the Jesuits who founded a college at Tyrnan, attempted to suppress Protestant worship, a policy which Rudolph determined to continue. Family feuds and his own illness impeded his efforts, however, and the Protestants were able to re-group under the protection of Bethlen Gabor, prince of the semi-independent province of Transylvania.

Not until the reign of Ferdinand II was further progress made, once again the vital period being the 1620s, when the Counter Reformation was inspired from within Hungary by the Jesuit and ex-protestant, Peter Pazmany, Archbishop of Gran from 1616 to 1637. Pazmany, a devout Roman Catholic and an ardent supporter of the Hapsburgs, attempted to achieve conversion by persuasion and since the nobility had little to lose and, politically, a great deal to gain by becoming Catholic, the policy proved successful. Seminaries for Hungarian priests were established in Vienna and in Rome and in 1637 a Catholic university was founded at Nagyszombat. Gradually the movement gained momentum, especially amongst the nobility, and the number of Protestants diminished as Pazmany insisted on a greater purity and higher standard of work and education from the priesthood. Hungary was never totally reconverted to Roman Catholicism but, by the middle of the seventeenth century, the majority of its population had returned to the Roman faith.

[18] SUCCESS AND FAILURE IN THE NORTH

Poland traditionally played a full part in the life of the western Church, and at the beginning of the sixteenth century its Church was less in need of reform than its counterparts in the west. Despite this the Protestant Reformation made considerable progress, first in the shape of Lutheranism and later of Calvinism and Anti-Trinitarianism. Lutheranism was essentially too Germanic, and racial tensions ensured that its success would be limited; moreover, the advent of Calvinism and Anti-Trinitarianism divided the Protestant movement and assisted the recovery of the Catholic Church.

The Church was also aided by the Polish monarchs of the sixteenth century who, although occasionally favouring the Protestants, never consistently supported their cause. Sigismund I (1506–48) was a firm Catholic but, as he grew older and his grip slackened, Lutheranism spread more easily. On the other hand his successor, Sigismund Augustus (1548–72), moved in the opposite direction. Tolerant and cultured, although often indecisive, he showed an early favour to the Protestants which was not maintained, and towards the end of his life he allowed important aspects of the Counter Reformation to be introduced, in particular the Trent decreees and the papal nuncio, Commendone. The short reign of the French King, Henry of Valois (1572–6), achieved little, except to focus Polish eyes on the horror of the massacre of St Bartholomew's Day, consequently increasing their determination to avoid such bloodshed in Poland. To this end, in 1573 the Diet decreed in a document known as the Confederation of Warsaw that:

As there is great discord in the kingdom touching the Christian religion, we promise, in order to avoid sedition such as has come to other kingdoms . . . that all of us of different religions will keep the peace between ourselves and shed no blood.

This tolerant spirit was maintained in the reign of Stephen Bathory (1576–86) who, although a devout Roman Catholic and a strong supporter of the Counter Reformation, affirmed even in the face of great opposition that the faith should be spread 'not by violence, fire and the sword, but by instruction and good example . . .'. Likewise Sigismund III (1587–1632), an equally devout Catholic, with interests in his ex-kingdom of Sweden as well as in Poland, adhered to a peaceful policy. From the middle of the sixteenth century, therefore, the monarchy gave consistent support to the Counter Reformation; nevertheless, the real impetus came from within the Polish Church itself.

John Laski (d. 1531), Archbishop of Gniezno, and Peter Tomicki (d. 1535), Bishop of Cracow having requested the pope to summon the General Council, endeavoured by their writings and by their exhortations to the clergy, to check the initial growth of Lutheranism. They achieved only limited success, however, and effective reform did not begin until after the middle of the century, when it centred around the life and work of Stanilas Hosius (d. 1579). Hosius, who began his writings against Luther in the 1520s, rose to be successively Bishop of Chelmno, Bishop of Ermland, papal nuncio and cardinal. As a bishop he held provincial synods to contest Lutheran and other Protestant views and to stress to the clergy the importance of action; he recommended the careful selection of bishops whom he encouraged to carry out strict visitations of their dioceses, and he urged that priests should be properly trained. His writings defending the Catholic Church inspired others to do the same and he used every conceivable means, inside and outside Poland, to spread his views. By his actions he achieved much, and by his example he helped to create the atmosphere in which others carried on the work which he had begun.

In 1551 the Synod of Pietrkow directed him to write the *Confession of the Catholic Faith* for which he became famous and in 1555, at Hosius's request, the papal nuncio, Lippomano visited Poland, touring every Polish see. Such was Hosius's reputation that, having been summoned to Rome in 1558, he was appointed papal nuncio to the imperial court at Vienna in 1560; two years later he presided over the third session of the Council of Trent. His standing with the Papacy enabled him to exert considerable influence on affairs within Poland. Consequently he arranged for John Commendone to go there as nuncio in 1563, taking with him the decrees of Trent, meeting Hosius's friends, particularly at the Synod of Ermland in 1565 which Hosius had organised, and gaining acceptance for the decrees. Furthermore in 1564, Hosius arranged for the Jesuits, headed by Christopher Strombelius, to visit Poland, which began a long and highly successful Jesuit presence in the country.

It would be wrong to give Hosius all the credit for the revival, for other leaders of the Church such as Bishop Kromer at Ermland, Kamkouski at Cuivia, later Archbishop of Gniezno, Solekowski at Livow and Cardinal Radziwell at Cracow did important work by holding frequent synods, by helping religious orders, by encouraging the Jesuits and by enforcing the Trent decrees, which were officially accepted by the bishops in 1577. Yet the spirit and energy of these men, together with the improved standard of the clergy owed much to Hosius himself for, although he never returned to Poland after 1569, his influence remained powerful, and his court at Rome became a centre for young men from Poland who returned to enter the Church.

The Polish monarchy, particularly under Bathory and Sigismund III, actively encouraged the revival which was further assisted by growing disunity amongst the Protestants, to such an extent that although Protestantism remained strong amongst the nobility and within the state assembly, from about the 1570s it ceased to grow. This was accentuated by the work of the Franciscans amongst the lower classes and by the rapid growth in Catholic education under the Jesuits.

Although Jesuits performed all kinds of services, their greatest contribution was undoubtedly in educating the upper and middle classes. Bathory supported them in the foundation and elevation of their colleges, the first being established in 1566 at Braunsberg, closely followed by others at Pultusk, Poznana and at Wilno where both the laity and priests were educated; soon they spread to Cracow, Riga and Polock, and Bathory raised the academy of Wilno into a full university. Thus between 1564 and 1610 they established twenty to thirty colleges in Poland, about 10,000 boys thereby receiving a Jesuit education. Even by 1586, there were 360 Jesuits in the country and Sigismund III, who was himself educated by them, continued Bathory's patronage.

Such pressure inevitably brought results. An increasing number of the nobility re-embraced the Catholic faith so that in 1598 the papal nuncio was able to write:

A short time ago, it might have been feared that heresy would
entirely supersede Catholicism in Poland. Now Catholicism is bearing
heresy to its grave.

The greatest achievement of the Counter Reformation in
Poland, however, was that its successes were accomplished
largely without bloodshed and violence for, from early in the
Reformation, the various faiths had implicitly agreed to use
persuasion rather than force, and this policy had been continued
by the monarchs and other leaders of society. In the last resort
Catholicism proved more acceptable to Poland than Protestantism because of its long and deep connection with Polish society,
where anti-clericalism and the corruption of the Church had
never been so marked as in the west. Thus by 1600 Poland was
virtually recovered thanks to the efforts of Poles like Hosius and
foreigners like the Jesuits and the papal nuncios; moreover, the
Church had been purified and a whole renaissance in Polish
theology and literature had occurred. The process was by no
means complete for many Protestants remained, but the trend
towards Catholicism continued and was not reversed, although
by the mid-seventeenth century a great deal of its energy had
been lost.

Poland also influenced other areas of northern and eastern
Europe. During the reign of Bathory missions were sent to
Livonia; a bishopric was set up at Wenden, Jesuits and priests
followed and the province was recovered for the Catholic
Church. Others entered the territories of the Orthodox Church in
eastern Poland, Russia, the Turkish Empire and the Middle
East. Success was limited, but the effort was a sound commentary
on the vitality of the Polish Church; moreover, in 1596 by the
Act of Brzese the Orthodox Church of east Poland acknowledged
the doctrine of the Catholic Church and the supremacy of the
Papacy, although retaining its own Slavonic rites and ceremonies.
Leaders of the Polish Counter Reformation were also interested
in Scandinavia, particularly in Sweden where Hosius made
contacts with John III. Under Sigismund the interest became
even greater.

Against Denmark and its dependent Norway the Counter Reformation achieved no success. The Catholic Church had been powerless to prevent the establishment of Lutheranism in Denmark in 1536 and in Norway in 1539, mainly because no Catholic prince was close or, at that time, strong enough to intervene. Not until the 1620s after Denmark's defeat at Lutter was there a possibility of attack, but Emperor Ferdinand's aims in north Germany were soon frustrated and the attempt came to nothing. Regarding Sweden, which also became Lutheran early in the sixteenth century, efforts were made although with little success. John III (1568–92), hoping to bring about a reconciliation between Lutherans and Catholics, produced his 'red book' containing details of a possible compromise, after which he contacted Hosius in Poland who arranged for two Jesuits to visit Sweden. Within Sweden, however, opposition mounted, especially since John's successor was to be Sigismund III of Poland, known to be a firm Catholic. Sigismund rarely visited Sweden during his reign (1592–9), and throughout the 1590s the Lutheran Church grew in strength under his uncle Charles, so much so that when Sigismund did land with an army in 1598 he was defeated, driven out and deposed in favour of Charles. Thereafter Sigismund never gave up hope of recovering Sweden and of reconverting it, but the timely and successful intervention of Charles's son, Gustavus Adolphus, into Polish affairs in 1621 and into German affairs in 1630 finally destroyed any such ideas.

[19] THE FINAL SUCCESS

The conflict between militant Calvinism and reformed Catholicism affected France earlier than in any other country, but the real flowering of the Catholic revival did not come about until the early seventeenth century, when, elsewhere, it was past its peak. From the death of Henry II in 1559 to the accession of Henry IV in 1589 France was plagued by a succession of weak

monarchs, who allowed various tensions to come to the surface
of French society which in turn produced a series of damaging
and protracted wars. Amongst these tensions was the issue of
religion. By the Concordat of Bologna, made with the Papacy in
1516, the French Crown gained political control of its Church,
but since both Francis I (1515–47) and Henry II (1547–59) were
preoccupied with other affairs, little reform was carried out so
that protests against the corruption and inefficiency of the
Church grew. Lutheranism appeared, but during the 1550s it
was largely replaced by Calvinism which, by 1559, accounted
for perhaps ten per cent of the population.

Although the Wars of Religion were primarily a power
struggle amongst the aristocracy, first for control of the crown
and, after 1584, for the crown itself, religion was firmly inter-
woven into the conflict for the Bourbons, centred on southern
France were mostly Calvinist, some for political, others for
genuinely religious reasons, while their rivals the Guise were the
foremost Catholic family in France (see Appendix IV).

The Inquisition was introduced into France in 1557 and the
Jesuits, having entered the country earlier, began teaching in
1564. Nevertheless the Guise remained the principal agents of
Catholicism for, despite their political aspirations, they were
devout Catholics opposed to any concessions being granted to
the Calvinists. Moreover, their power, centred in eastern France
and on Paris itself, was usually backed by the might of Spain.
Charles, Cardinal of Lorraine, an important figure at the third
session of the Council of Trent, returned to France in 1563
aiming to enforce the Council's decrees. Thus after the death of
his brother Francis, he led the struggle against both Calvinist
and Bourbon. For the purpose of defence he began the grouping
of parish churches into Catholic Leagues which, during the
1570s and 1580s, became extremely powerful. Meanwhile as
the wars hardened Catholic opinion the religious orders became
more active. The Feuillants founded as an austere branch of the
Cistercians by the Abbot Jean de la Barrière in 1577, the
Capucins and the Jesuits strove to counter the spread of Calvinism, at the same time as a Jesuit, Robert Bellarmine, con-

fronted during the 1580s by the prospect of a Calvinist becoming king, prepared a justification of rebellion to an ungodly monarch.

Despite the growth of Guise power in the 1580s the Calvinist, Henry of Navarre, did succeed to the throne in 1589. By 1593 he had won acceptance in most of France but, since the wars had concentrated Calvinism in the south-west, where a virtually autonomous republic was established, Henry was forced to accept the faith of the majority of Frenchmen and to receive instruction in Catholicism. It was therefore, as a Roman Catholic, absolved by Clement VIII, that he was crowned in 1594. Thereafter, despite the Edict of Nantes in 1598, the monarchy remained Catholic.

In spite of this great success the state of the French Roman Catholic Church remained poor. In addition, there were other complications for the spirit of the Counter Reformation was predominantly Italian and Spanish, yet a strong Gallican tradition remained in France which disapproved of both influences. For this reason the crown never officially accepted the decrees of Trent and received the Jesuits with grave mistrust although they provided confessors to Henry IV, Louis XIII and Louis XIV.

St Vincent de Paul (1576–1660), the last great figure of the Counter Reformation, wrote, 'Christianity depends on the priests. Priests living in the manner most do today are the greatest enemies of God's Church.' Thus by the reign of Henry IV (1589–1610), devout Frenchmen realised that, until the quality of the French clergy was improved, little could be done to raise the standard of instruction provided for the mass of the French people. Local priests were often as uneducated as the peasantry to whom they ministered, while the higher clergy many of whom, like Cardinal Mazarin, led scandalous lives, were normally political appointees. Thus the gulf between the lower clergy and the hierarchy was complete.

Nonetheless there were examples of politically appointed bishops carrying out their duties conscientiously. Although Richelieu inherited the bishopric of Luçon in 1602 at the age of seventeen with no wish even to enter the Church, he applied himself to the task by disciplining the clergy and by undertaking frequent visitations of the diocese, so much so that he was considered a future champion of the Counter Reformation. As such he was chosen to present the clergy's address to the 1614 Estates General.

It was not until later, however, that clerical standards were generally improved and then it was largely due to the efforts of various individuals, amongst the first of whom were Bérulle (1575–1629) and his cousin Madame Acarie (1566–1618). Both, having been deeply influenced by the work of the Spanish mystics, determined to contact other devout Catholics and to organise active groups throughout France. For this purpose Bérulle founded the French Oratory in 1611. Containing both laymen and clergy it set an excellent example to the priesthood by its works of charity and devotion. Meanwhile Madame Acarie made her house a centre for discussion and for the planning of other charitable schemes.

Without doubt the most important figure in raising the standards of the French clergy and in taking the Christian message to common people was St Vincent de Paul; a man of many parts. Born of poor parents and educated by the Franciscans, he was captured by Barbary pirates and sold into slavery in Tunis. Having converted his master and escaped to Europe, he became chaplain and friend to the powerful Gondi family, yet he never lost sight of his humble origins. In 1625, backed by the wealth of the Gondi family, he founded the Congregation of the Mission, commonly known as Lazarists from the original house at Saint-Lazaire; by 1700 there were fifty-three houses. Their purpose was to train and educate priests to go into backward rural areas and to encourage country priests themselves to take courses at their houses. Over 800 missions, usually working in teams, emanated from St Vincent's foundation and, in turn, seminaries for the training of priests were set up elsewhere. At Richelieu's request St Vincent supervised the first of these and by 1660 400 priests were being produced every year; each taught above all, to see the importance of pastoral work and to stress the Christian message of love. Women like

Madame Acarie and men like St Vincent also succeeded in making charity fashionable. Thus in 1617 St Vincent founded the Filles de Charité for women who were prepared to work in hospitals and amongst the poor.

St Francis de Sales (1567–1622) was another fine example of the devotion newly found within the French Church. Like Bérulle and St Vincent he combined personal mysticism with a life of action, working chiefly in south-eastern France and in Switzerland around Chablais. Supported by the Duke of Savoy, consecrated Bishop of Geneva in 1602 yet working under the eyes of the Calvinist leaders, St Francis endured unbelievable hardship to take the Catholic faith to the people of that area. In his writings and in his work he was an inspiration to others, especially to women for whom, with Jeanne de Chantral, he founded the Order of the Visitations in 1610, a society which enabled women without the physical strength for a full monastic life to participate in devotion and in charitable works; by 1641 the order possessed eighty-six houses. His books, *An introduction to the devout life*, published in 1609 and a *Treatise of Divine Love* of 1616 attempted to explain how a man, living in the world, with its evils and its temptations, could nevertheless dwell in the presence of God. The process for the canonisation of St Francis began only four years after his death – a fitting tribute to the wonderful example he provided for all who met or who knew of him.

The work of the new orders, although vital, must not obscure either the revival which took place in older orders including the Franciscans, Dominicans, Feuillants and Benedictines, or the importance of the activities of the Jesuits. Despite their banishment between 1594 and 1603, they made continuous progress, two Jesuits, Auger and Regis, being amongst the first, at the end of the sixteenth century, to take the Christian gospel to poor country parishes. Although they maintained their interest in this kind of work, their principal importance rested with education. They established a college in the Palace of St Clement in Paris which was followed by others at Lyon and at Dijon, where the sons of the upper classes received a thorough education.

Many of the young men who passed through their hands carried on private works of charity helping in the foundation of other new orders, of which the most important was the Company of the Holy Sacrament founded in 1630 by the Duc de Ventadour. By 1658 the company possessed fifty-two branches dedicated not merely to charitable activities but to isolating the Huguenots and to watching the morals and behaviour of the highest within society. In their methods, particularly in the use of pamphlets and propaganda, and in their energy they were true disciples of the Jesuits. Despite continuous mistrust of the order the Jesuits provided confessors to every French monarch of the seventeenth century but, from about 1640 onwards, they became bitterly involved in the dispute over Jansenism, which helped to increase dislike of the society and its methods.

Jansenism originated in the work of Cornelius Jansen (d. 1638), a Flemish theologian, who placed great emphasis on the writings of St Augustine. His book *Augustinus* was not published until 1640, but his views were taken up in France by his friend Saint-Cyran and centred on the communities of quietists at Port Royal which, under the patronage of the Arnould family, sought a closer relationship with God shorn of excessive ceremony and symbolism. Basically the dispute, involving the freedom of the human will, was as old as Christianity itself. Jansen believed in a form of predestination, teaching that because of man's inability to influence God's designs he could do little to bring about his own salvation. The Jesuits, on the other hand, argued that since man was able to influence God by good works, he therefore possessed a considerable degree of free will. The Dominicans, who had long argued with the Jesuits on this very question, took a middle line. During the 1650s the tone, and also the bitterness, of the dispute was raised by the intervention of Pascal who, in his *Lettres Provinciales* of 1656, supported the Jansensists. After 1660 Louis XIV attempted to produce a compromise but without success and, as Jansenism took on political overtones, it, and the settlement at Port Royal, was destroyed early in the eighteenth century.

Thus, the Wars of Religion having ensured that France would

remain Catholic, a renaissance occurred within the French Church during the first half of the seventeenth century which carried the whole Counter Reformation movement to its final peak. Although the Monarchy had given only limited support the revival greatly strengthened its prestige; indeed Louis XIV, attempting to enlarge royal authority by enforcing religious uniformity, banished the Huguenot minority by withdrawing the Edict of Nantes in 1685.

The outburst of enthusiasm which permeated the Church from the middle of the sixteenth century found unlimited opportunities in the new lands discovered by Europeans throughout the world. The same zeal which had brought about reform of the Spanish Church under Ferdinand and Isabella accompanied the Conquistadores to the Americas (see page 49) while, in 1540, John III of Portugal requested the Jesuits to follow Portuguese explorers and traders to India and the Far East. Thus it was that St Francis Xavier (1506–52), the greatest of all Jesuit missionaries, left for India in 1542. Landing at Goa, he worked his way south to the fisherman's coast of Coromandel where

He went up and down the streets and squares with a bell in his hand, crying to the children and others to come to the instructions. The novelty of the proceeding, never before seen in Goa, brought a large crowd around him which he then led to the church. He began by singing the lessons which he had rhymed and then made the children sing them so that they might become the better fixed in their memories. Afterwards he explained each point in the simplest way, using only such words as his young audience could readily understand. By this method, which has since been adopted everywhere in the Indies, he so deeply ingrained the truths and concepts of the faith in the hearts of the people that men and women, children and old folk, took to singing the Ten Commandments while they walked the streets, as did the fisherman in his boat and the labourer in the fields, for their own entertainment and recreation.

In 1599 Goa was made the seat of a Catholic archbishopric while, on the fisherman's coast Xavier had achieved lasting success, the area being divided by 1600 into sixteen large villages each supervised by a Jesuit Father.

Further inland the Jesuit Aquavivi made contact in 1580 with Akbar, the Mogul Emperor, but, although a presence was maintained at his court, no major conversion was achieved. In 1605 there arrived in southern India perhaps the most remarkable Jesuit missionary of all. Robert de Nobili, who lived for fifty years in the area of Madurai adopting Indian dress and even mastering Sanskrit, was bitterly criticised at home for his concessions to native customs and for his methods; nevertheless by the time of his death at Mylapore in 1656, in blindness and in poverty, he had won an enormous number of converts. He failed, however, to create a sufficient number of Indian priests and too many of his converts were from the lower castes, yet his was an amazing achievement which helped to consolidate Christianity in south-west India.

Meanwhile missionaries pushed further east. In 1649 Xavier and two other Jesuits, having passed through the Moluccas, arrived in Japan where they set up a mission which, in the years that followed, and long after Xavier's departure on new ventures, made such progress, even amongst local rulers, that in 1579 Alessandir Valignano, Director of Jesuit operations in the East, visited Japan to help in its organisation. He decreed that Christianity should be adapted to suit local customs and furthermore that Japanese converts should be accepted into the priesthood. Thus, in 1601, the first Japanese were ordained by which time there were reckoned to be 300,000 baptised Christians in Japan. Thereafter, however, disaster struck as the Shogun Emperors began a systematic persecution in which, between 1614 and 1630, sixty-two Europeans were martyred, together with nearly 2,000 Japanese, resulting in the total destruction of Christianity.

Having taken the mission to Japan, Xavier looked eagerly towards China but, in 1552, he died on the island of Sancian while in sight of his goal. Consequently, the mission to China was founded by another Jesuit, Matthew Ricci (1552–1610) who, setting out from Portuguese Macao in 1579 gained entry to the imperial court at Peking in 1600, where he won favour by his ability to keep working the clocks presented to the Emperor and by his willingness to adapt his methods to Chinese customs. Carefully fusing Christianity with the Confucian system he steadily made converts both in the court, although not the Emperor himself, and in the rest of China, until at his death in 1610 there were about 2,000 Christians centred on Shanghai, Chekiang and Hanchow. Ricci's successor was a German Jesuit, Johann Adam Schall von Bell (1591–1666), who continued his work so successfully that it outlived the Ming dynasty, which fell in 1662. In 1674 a Chinese, Lo Wen-Tsao, was consecrated bishop and the mission continued into the eighteenth century, by which time the Jesuits had translated into Chinese all the main liturgical works of the Catholic faith.

In 1579 a bishopric was set up at Manila for the Philippines which, by 1700, were almost totally converted; an achievement which has endured. Strenuous efforts were made in Siam although without result, but the mission to Vietnam, having run into various difficulties, established itself thanks to the work of Alexander de Rhodes. Despite his expulsion in 1645 conversions were made and in the south the Church survived.

In Africa, little success was achieved, although missionaries established themselves early on in coastal stations. By 1624 the Jesuits had eight outposts in Mozambique and about twenty missionaries in the Zambezi area but to no avail; affairs were too confused and the tribes not sufficiently advanced, and so the conversion of Africa was delayed for another two centuries.

Despite the earlier work of the Spanish in the Americas (see page 49) considerable problems remained. In 1610 Jesuits led missions to Paraguay where, by 1623, twenty-three settlements were established, but they had few roots since no native priests were ordained; consequently, during the eighteenth century, when the Jesuits were expelled, the settlement collapsed. Further north, in Peru, Central America, Mexico and the Caribbean, the work of the early Spanish missionaries was successfully consolidated although, as in Paraguay, the lack of native priests proved to be an obstacle. In North America the French made efforts to convert the Iroquois and Huron Indians of Canada. Led by the Jesuits and the Ursulines, the missionaries worked mostly in the area of Montreal but to no effect, for, by 1650, after considerable loss of life including some fearsome martyrdoms, the mission had to be abandoned.

Confronted by the varied activities of the missionaries, Gregory XV, realising the need for central supervision, established the Congregation for the Propagation of the Faith in 1622. Its first secretary, Francesco Ingoli, did the vital job of coordinating the work of the missions until 1649, thereby building up a wealth of information on their activities. By a decree drawn up in 1659 the Congregation also settled the dispute concerning the extent to which the missionaries should accept local customs:

Do not regard it as your task, and do not bring any pressure to bear on the peoples, to change their manners, customs, and uses, unless they are evidently contrary to religion and sound morals. . . . Do not introduce all that to them, but only the faith, which does not despise or destroy the manners and customs of any people. . . . Do not draw invidious contrasts between the customs of the peoples and those of Europe; do your utmost to adapt yourselves to them.

The bare details of the missionary work cannot pay adequate tribute to the devotion and bravery of those, not only Jesuits, who carried it out. Such men accepted not only the risk of torture or martyrdom in foreign lands, but also the dangers of the journey itself; indeed between 1581 and 1712, of the 367 Jesuits who sailed for China, 127 died on the voyage.

In every phase of the Counter Reformation the Jesuits played a major role, for under their first three generals, Loyola (1540–56), Lainez (1556–65) and Francis Borgia (1565–72), they set standards which both laymen and clergy sought to follow. To their mystical devotions, they allied lives of action stiffened by an iron resolve produced in years of vigorous training, which taught utter obedience to their general and to the pope, and from which only the fittest survived. As members of a great society they gained confidence, and by the terms of their charter they gained mobility and flexibility. Wherever they journeyed they adapted themselves to the needs of the situation, whether in the slums of Italy, amongst the peasants of India or in the greatest courts of Europe. Feared, despised and hated by opponents throughout Europe, they were, nevertheless, the Papacy's most effective weapons, especially through their control of education.

Answering the demand for education in sixteenth-century Europe, they established seminaries for the education of priests and colleges and universities for laymen, mostly of the upper and middle classes. Thus they created a generation of young men, many from the royal households of Europe to whom they later became confessors, schooled in Catholicism. In addition, they helped in the founding of colleges at Rome to train exiles from Protestant nations. Throughout this period the society prospered, so that by 1556 at Loyola's death the original small band had become over 1,000; by 1600 13,112 and by 1773, when for a time it was dissolved, it numbered 22,589.

Despite this the most important figures in enforcing the Counter Reformation were the secular princes. In the last resort even the Jesuits were fighting a losing battle where the government had firmly turned to Protestantism. Occasionally, future rulers, such as Emperor Rudolph II, Maximilian of Bavaria or Emperor Ferdinand II could be swayed by a Catholic education and, where, as in Poland, the situation was in the balance, a ruler might be persuaded to accept the Catholic Church, nevertheless it was ultimately the ruler who decided.

Principal Events

Spain

1530s.	Suppression of Erasmians and Illuminists
1547.	Purity of blood made necessary for holding church offices
1558.	Prohibition on the import of foreign books
1559.	Restrictions on students studying abroad
	Revision of the Index
1559–76.	Carranza dispute
1568.	Special restrictions for Catalonia
1560s ⎫ 1570s ⎭	*Golden age of the Spanish Church*
	1562. Discaled Carmelites founded at Avila by St Teresa
	1572. Hospitaller Brothers officially founded
1588.	Failure of the Armada

The Netherlands

1550s.	Introduction of the Council of Blood (the Inquisition)
1556.	Introduction of the Jesuits
1564.	Introduction of the Trent decrees
1567–73.	Alvà's reign of terror
1572.	Outbreak of the Revolt
1578–92.	Governorship of Parma and reconquest of the southern provinces
1596–1621.	Archduke Albert governor of the southern provinces
	Reconstruction of Roman Catholicism

England

1553–8.	Catholic reaction under Mary
1559.	Elizabeth's Protestant settlement
1568.	College for English priests founded at Douai by William Allen
1570.	Excommunication of Elizabeth
1574.	First Douai priests arrive in England
1580.	First Jesuits arrive
1588.	Armada
1605.	Gunpowder Plot

Portugal
1531.   Introduction of the Inquisition
1540.   Introduction of the Jesuits
           Departure of Xavier for the Far East

Germany
1555.   Peace of Augsburg
           Lutheranism accepted in the Empire
1540s ⎫
1550s ⎭   Introduction of the Jesuits

           1544. Cologne
           1551. Vienna
           1556. Prague
           1559. Munich
Leadership provided by Wittelsbach rulers of Bavaria
           1550–79.   Albert V
           1579–97.   William V
           1597–1651. Maximilian I
1582.   Catholic victory at the Diet over the Protestant Arch-
           bishop of Magdeburg
           Catholic victory over Gebhard Truchsess, Archbishop of
           Cologne
1580s ⎫   Catholic progresss in north-west, central and southern
1590s ⎭   Germany
1608.   Donauworth incident
1609.   Formation of the Roman Catholic League
           Cleves-Julich dispute
1618–48.   Thirty Years' War
           1620–3. Palatinate overrun by Catholic forces
           1629.   Edict of Restitution
           1635.   Peace of Prague – Edict of Restitution with-
                    drawn
           1648.   Peace of Westphalia

Austria
1564–1637. Reform in Inner Austria instigated by Hapsburg
           Archdukes
           1564–90.   Archduke Charles
           1595–1637. Archduke Ferdinand
1619–37.   Reform in Austria as a whole under Emperor Ferdinand II

Bohemia

1609.	The Letters of Majesty granted
1617.	Ferdinand of Styria elected king
1618.	Revolt
1620.	Rebels defeated at the battle of the White Mountain
1620–7.	Roman Catholicism reimposed

Poland

The monarchy remains Catholic and gives the lead

1506–48.	Sigismund I
1548–72.	Sigismund II Augustus
1572–6.	Henry of Valois
1576–86.	Stephen Bathory
1587–1632.	Sigismund III

1551.	*Confession of the Catholic Faith* written by Hosius
1555.	The papal nuncio Lippomano tours Poland
1563.	Commendone appointed papal nuncio
	Introduction of the Trent decrees
1564.	Introduction of the Jesuits

France

1559.	Death of Henry II
1561.	Colloquy of Poissy – failure to reach religious compromise
1562.	Outbreak of the Wars of Religion
1572.	Massacre of St Bartholomew's day
1570s 1580s }	Development of Catholic Leagues
1584.	Treaty of Joinville between Spain and the League
1589.	A Protestant, Henry of Navarre, becomes King
1593.	Conversion of Henry to Roman Catholicism
1598.	Edict of Nantes
1611.	French Oratory founded by Bérulle
1567–1622.	Life of St Francis de Sales
	1602. Appointed bishop of Geneva
	1609. *Introduction to the devout life* written
	1616. *Treatise of divine love* written
1576–1660.	Life of St Vincent de Paul
	1625. Foundation of the Lazarists
	1620s 1630s } Foundation of colleges to train priests

Overseas missionary work

1542.	Departure of Xavier for India
1549.	Xavier begins the mission to Japan
1579.	Roman Catholic bishopric established at Manila in the Philippines
1580.	The Jesuit Aquaviva visits the Mogul emperor
1600.	The Jesuit Ricci establishes himself at the Imperial court of China
1622.	Establishment of the Congregation for the Propagation of the Faith

Conclusions

The vitality of the Counter Reformation and the piety and devotion which it inspired were remarkable achievements, especially since it was never a fully united movement for, even during the periods of greatest success, in the 1580s and 1590s and again in the 1620s, serious divisions existed.

Although the Papacy gave the all-important lead at Trent, it was forced to rely upon other agents to enforce the decrees, and with those agents it was not always in agreement, particularly when they were great princes. Quarrels inevitably arose which prevented the movement taking an even, much less a uniform course; nowhere was this better illustrated than in the confused attitude towards the English heresy in the first years of the reign of Elizabeth. Similarly, the religious orders, who did so much to take revived Catholicism to the people of Europe, often wrangled bitterly amongst themselves. Above all, the Jesuits and the Dominicans clashed on a variety of issues, ranging from the jealousy of an old and long-established order for a new and, it seemed, dangerously unorthodox one, to academic arguments on the extent of man's free will. Furthermore, none of the orders was well liked by the secular clergy, whose work they often seemed to be doing and from whom they took both praise and prestige. The educational standard of the clergy remained low but, as contemporaries pointed out, this was likely to be perpetuated as long as the orders themselves took so many of the most promising young men.

Despite these divisions the movement made great progress in which the popes, princes, religious orders and secular clergy shared. Nor must the importance of the papal nuncios be overlooked; in Germany and Poland especially they introduced papal policies into the highest places at the appropriate moment.

Although the Church became increasingly Italian in character

Spanish influence was also vital to the spread of the Counter Reformation. The Armada, the attempted suppression of heresy in the Netherlands, and the purification of the Spanish Church itself are well known, but the influence extended much further. Even after the death of Loyola the Jesuits retained a distinctive Spanish flavour which they carried throughout Europe and the New Worlds, while in a later generation the mystical writings of St Teresa and her circle had an impact far beyond the boundaries of Spain itself. Nor did the Spanish monarchy forget its duty towards its Austrian cousins; Philip II constantly prodded and cajoled them into action, to such an extent that there arose in the imperial courts at Prague and Vienna a 'Spanish party' dedicated, amongst other things, to the reimposition of orthodoxy in the Hapsburg lands of south-east Europe. Emperor Rudolph II was even educated in the Spanish court, while Ferdinand II retained close links with Spain – often, it was felt, to the detriment of the imperial cause. Not even the popes could feel entirely free from Spanish direction, particularly in the need for political cooperation in northern Italy, and against the Turks in the Mediterranean.

Without doubt, the attitude of the prince was the deciding factor in the success or failure of the Church's revival, and no European country returned to Catholicism against the wishes of its ruler. Whether a prince supported or opposed the Counter Reformation depended on a mixture of religious, political and economic motives. Some rulers were undoubtedly deeply pious men. By education and upbringing, Philip II, Ferdinand II, Maximilian of Bavaria and Sigismund III of Poland were amongst those devout Catholics who, while not always in the first instance prepared to sacrifice the interests of the state, were anxious to advance the Church. But this was by no means all that was involved. Above all, secular rulers were concerned with their political authority, so severely challenged by free cities, elected assemblies and popular revolt that often they used the Church as a means of buttressing their power.

After the 1560s Lutheranism, which upheld the authority of

monarchy, lost its vitality and the active Protestant movement largely centred around Calvinism which offered little support to secular rulers. On the other hand, the Counter Reformation Church stood for the preservation of the existing social order. Trent confirmed its hierarchical organisation and maintained its superior position in society by insisting that men could find God only through its organisation. Moreover, through its law courts and the confessional, the Church possessed considerable coercive powers throughout Catholic countries, not merely near the centres of government – a vital weapon in the struggle to maintain law and order. It is not surprising therefore that rulers of the late sixteenth and seventeenth centuries, seeking to extend the effectiveness of their governments, turned readily to the conservative forces of the Church.

Although Rome would not countenance theories of royal supremacy over national churches, it did usually allow individual princes the power of episcopal appointment. In this way, the Catholic Church and absolute government came to be identified in the struggle against heresy and rebellion. This was certainly the case in southern Germany, the southern Netherlands and in the lands of the Austrian Hapsburgs where reconversion and the extension of royal government became one and the same process.

The notion that absolute government and revived Catholicism took root most easily in societies which were rural, or backward in technological and economic development, and lacking in organised and legal means of dissent, is open to considerable doubt. It may be that this type of society was the result rather than the cause of such success. In Brabant and Flanders a long tradition of urban privilege and dissent existed, yet they remained within the Catholic Netherlands; similarly Bohemia, with its Hussite tradition and city of Prague, was not a docile area. Austria itself possessed considerable dissent, and even separatist movements, as well as a large urban community in its capital Vienna. In Ireland and perhaps Poland the social and intellectual conditions may have favoured the Counter Reformation, but elsewhere, as in France, the pattern was more complicated. The social, economic and intellectual structures clearly did matter, but geography was also important; most decisive, however, was the attitude of the ruling prince and the availability of military force to impose his will.

Nevertheless where the forces of Catholicism and absolute monarchy did triumph, a conservative and aristocratic society often resulted. In the southern Netherlands, this is evident by contrast with the United Provinces, and the same is true of Bavaria, the Austrian Hapsburg Empire and Spain but France falls into no particular category and serves as a warning against over simplified theories.

The Council of Trent began a process which, in the course of less than a century, modernised the Catholic Church and left it in a shape which has lasted almost until the present day. The confirmation of papal supremacy was the most important decision but this was only the prelude. The basic structure of the medieval Church remained unaltered, but it was given a higher degree of organisation to enable it to deal with its sixteenth and seventeenth-century problems. The cardinals were organised into a form of advisory cabinet, separate departments were formally established to carry on the papal business, and diplomatic activities were expanded by the creation of many more permanent nuncios, especially in Germany. Rebuilding programmes returned the city of Rome, and St Peter's in particular, to its former grandeur. The religious orders worked within the world rather than withdrawing from it and the medieval ideal of withdrawal and contemplation never found favour within the Counter Reformation, even amongst its mystics.

The process of centralisation was seen also in the careful definition of doctrine carried out at Trent. Many still disagreed or believed that there was room for debate, but on important issues the Church made its attitude clear, and Catholics could rarely be in doubt as to what represented orthodoxy. Connected with this was the greater emphasis placed on education. The Jesuits educated the Catholic laity as well as their own novices and, although very slow to take effect, the seminaries established at the third session of Trent, gradually raised the standard of the priesthood. The extended powers given to the bishops, however, probably comprised the greatest process of modernisation, and this may well be the principal reason why, in those areas where the Catholic Church regained its position, it managed to retain such a firm hold on society.

By 1700 the extra power which Trent deliberately gave to the bishops had taken effect. Following the lines of Borromeo's work in Milan, many dioceses were run like efficient military organisations, in which any challenge to orthodoxy, uniformity or episcopal authority was effectively dealt with. Examples may be taken from all over Catholic Europe to illustrate how bishops enforced a uniform observance of orthodox rites and practices. Family feuds which prevented many from attending church were looked into, the independence of fraternities was attacked, early baptism was insisted upon and children were given catechisms from which to learn the basic tenets of the faith. In all this the Catholic bishops were more efficient than their Protestant counterparts.

Beneath the modernisation, the piety and the devotion, however, lay faults which contained the seeds of future decline. Trent had declared the doctrine so definitely that the flexibility of the medieval Church was lost. It was less possible for individuals or groups to hold differing views and yet still to remain orthodox; a uniformity had been laid down which, by the very success of its administrative reforms, the Church was more able to enforce than ever before. Even more important, at Trent the Church turned its back on a number of developments which might have made it more acceptable to later generations.

The Protestant Reformation had raised the issue of participation by the congregation in church affairs, but this had been rejected, and the increasing number of educated laity found themselves unable to influence the Church. In an age when vernacular languages were developing rapidly, the Church chose to retain Latin for its services and for its Bible. Similarly, the humanists, including many staunch Catholics, had vigorously pressed that biblical studies should play a greater part in the education of the clergy, but again the Church proved conservative and retained its traditional scholastic methods. The Counter Reformation Church continued to lay emphasis on the ecstasies of the saints, on miracles performed at shrines and on the celebration of the numerous saints' days. Such trends, together with the activities of the Inquisition and the Index, provided an atmosphere which was not conducive to a reliance on reason or an enquiring mind. The Church, insisting on standing as an intermediary between God and man, left little to the activity or thought of the individual and this ultimately left it rigid and exposed in the face of the scientific Renaissance of the seventeenth century and the scepticism of the educated laity of the eighteenth century. Congregations were required to follow blindly and while, for peasantry and lesser folk, this provided the security and leadership which they needed, for others it proved unsatisfactory.

The Church's attitude to the advances in science and philosophy was extremely confused. Galileo did most of his work in Italy and a great deal of the medical researches of Harvey and others were also carried on there. During the seventeenth century, societies were established for the advancement of science by Prince Cesi in 1603 at Rome and by Ferdinand of Tuscany in 1653, but these were the exceptions. The Sacred College in Rome condemned the Copernican beliefs of Galileo in 1616, and in 1632 his views were declared 'contrary to holy scripture' and incompatible with the Christian faith. The structure of the Church's theology still rested on an Aristotelian concept of the universe, to such an extent that it could not allow such basic suppositions to be questioned. In Spain also, the study of science was severely curtailed, and although intellectual activity was not confined to Protestant countries it is nevertheless true that the great progress of the seventeenth and eighteenth centuries belonged to northern Europe and, in particular, to the Protestant states of England, Scotland, the United Provinces and parts of Germany.

In general, Catholic political theorists adhered to the doctrine of non-resistance. The Church had traditionally taught that a people had no right of rebellion against an unpopular ruler and clearly, in the sixteenth and seventeenth centuries when Church and monarchy were often allied in their struggles, it was essential that this doctrine be maintained. In France the Church went so far as to support the theory of the divine right of kings. There were dissident voices, however, and, amongst others, certain Jesuits began to propound opposite views. Foremost amongst these were two Spanish Jesuits, Juan de Mariana (1535–1623) and Francisco Suarez (1548–1617).

Mariana, the most extreme, argued that royal power derived from a contract between the ruler and his subjects, and that ultimate authority rested with the people, usually represented in an assembly. It followed therefore that a prince might be deposed if he ruled in a manner which did not benefit the community, and Mariana pushed his argument to its logical conclusion by accepting, under certain conditions, the right of tyrannicide. He was particularly interested in the assassination of Henry III of France in 1589, which he considered justified. His contemporary Suarez, a lawyer by training, never sanctioned tyrannicide, but believed, with Mariana, that since society was a human creation for human needs, the origin of the power of a ruler was itself human and not divine. On the other hand the pope, who derived his authority directly from God, was the watchdog of the spiritual and moral health of the Christian nations, and in consequence it was natural that he should possess power, even though indirect, over the separate princes. This theory of papal supremacy was held also by the Italian Jesuit, Robert Bellarmine (1542–1621), who, accepting that the Papacy had no direct right of interference in the secular affairs of the state, believed that a pope might depose a ruler for heresy, or for offending against the moral teachings of the Church.

These Jesuits renewed the claims of the medieval Papacy, but they did so in the sixteenth century context. In an age when different Christian Churches appeared in Europe, it was inevitable that theories denying the divine right of kings and royal supremacy over the Church should be propounded. Nor were the Jesuits alone in this; faced by considerable royal opposition in England, France and the Netherlands the Calvinists produced similar theories of contract.

These Jesuit teachings were not typical of the whole Church, but they are important in the development of European political thought. Ultimately they produced results far from those for which the Jesuits hoped. By denying royal supremacy they implied that the Church should stand independent of the state; as this came about in the late seventeenth and eighteenth centuries the Church lost the support of the coercive powers of the secular government which had been a vital force in its sixteenth and seventeenth-century revival.

The Counter Reformation had considerable impact on the arts although not always in the manner usually suggested. The Baroque is a style generally associated with the revived Church but its magnificence and ostentation hardly fitted in with the austere and self-effacing spirit of Loyola, Carafa and the other earlier saints. Their spirit was best captured in the music of Palestrina (1526–94), the Choir Master of St Peter's, and of his friend Vittoria (1540–1611), a Spaniard living in Rome. These men wrote exclusively for the Church and Palestrina, in particular, produced music unsurpassed for its atmosphere of spiritual serenity. Their music served as a supplement to the liturgy of the services and as an accompaniment to ceremonial, without allowing itself to indulge in emotionalism. Palestrina wrote 105 masses in all, while few compositions caught the mystical spirit of the Counter Reformation saints as accurately as the 'Offices of Holy Week' written in 1585 by Vittoria.

The third session of Trent had considered abolishing church music but relented in a decree which insisted that it should not upset the ear or do anything to distract attention from the service. It was declared essential that the words should be clearly and audibly sung so that they could be understood. Music, therefore, was permitted to play a large part in the Counter Reformation although, except in Rome, the pure ideals of Palestrina and Vittoria were not long maintained, as missionaries used music to attract the wavering to church, and the more magnificent style of the Baroque appeared in the seventeenth century.

The austerity of the early years of the Counter Reformation as portrayed in music did not appear to the same extent in architecture or painting which were passing through the uninspiring stage known as Mannerism. In this period architects, and especially painters, sought, either to copy the greatness of the Renaissance masters, or simply to outdo them by startling innovations. Rome itself produced little art of value in the second half of the sixteenth century and it was not until virtually a second Renaissance overtook the city in the first half of the seventeenth century that a revival took place. It was in this Baroque age that the spirit of the Counter Reformation played an important part; it no longer represented the austere spirit of the early reformers but the lavish and extravagant style of a Church which had regained its confidence and which wished to commemorate its saints and their achievements.

The Venetian, Tintoretto (1518–94) and El Greco (1541–1614), working in Spain, both used religion for their themes, and each made an important contribution to the early development. Tintoretto portrayed episodes from the Bible with a new life and vigour, almost as if he felt the increased energy which circulated through the Church itself. Like El Greco his work was almost impressionistic as in 'The finding of St Mark's remains'. El Greco exhibited a profound feeling for human dignity, while accepting man's subordinate relationship to God; this facet of Counter Reformation thought, found elsewhere in the writings of the Spanish and French mystics, can be seen in his 'Burial of Count Orgaz' or his portrait of 'Brother Hortensio Felix Paravicino'.

The most important of the Baroque school in Rome were Michelangelo de Caravaggio (1565–1610), and Annibale Carraci (1560–1609). Carraci searched for the gentleness and charm of Raphael, and to this he added the emotion and sensuality of the Baroque. In 'The Virgin mourning Christ' he painted a religious topic which emphasised the emotion and the quiet human dignity of the situation. Caravaggio tried to paint his religious figures as they really were and to impress upon his audience the reality of religious situations; often this led to ugliness, as in the case of his 'Doubting Thomas', but never to lack of effect. In northern Europe the greatest figure was Peter Paul Rubens (1577–1640) who, having studied in Rome, did most of his painting in Antwerp. Although never a member of any particular school, his work is representative of the Baroque and he was patronised by Jesuits and Catholic rulers alike. He painted religious scenes on a grand scale, imparting to them a life and vigour of their own, and never failing to express the dignity of man.

The combination of respect for God and for the dignity of man appears also in architecture, although the style is flamboyant and not representative of the spirit of the early Counter Reformation. Rome was the focal point and Bernini the great figure. The first sign of a new life and style appeared in the church of Il Gesù, built for the Jesuits in Rome by Giacomo della Porte in 1575. The interior design was rectangular, which focused the attention of the congregation upon the altar, while on either side of the nave separate chapels were constructed for private worship; the façade also broke many contemporary rules and its complex design focused attention on the main doorway. These ideas were taken up by Bernini (1598–1680), Borromini (1599–1667) and others who were swamped by commissions from Roman patrons, including popes and cardinals, who wished to commemorate the saints of the Counter Reformation in elaborate buildings. As in painting, an effort was made to express grandeur with discipline and sensuality with faith; to combine the confidence of the reformed Church with its piety. Borromini's first important work was the church of San Carlo alle Quattro Fontane, which he began in 1633. The stage, however, was chiefly held by Bernini.

The main building of St Peter's had been completed in 1590, but in 1624 Urban VIII, himself a great patron of the arts, appointed Bernini to complete the final decorations and surrounding areas. He built the huge baldachino which rests over the high altar, and the piazza outside St Peter's with its magnificent colonnades which provides such a grand and satisfying setting to the church itself. Throughout the first half of the seventeenth century a wave of building continued in Rome in which magnificently conceived and ornately decorated churches glorified the revival of the Church. Bernini's talents were by no means confined to architecture, and as a sculptor his 'Ecstasy of St Teresa' epitomises more than any other single work the spirit of Catholic art in the Baroque age. The figures are dignified, well formed and attractive and yet the moment of mystic revelation is caught in the features.

It was a tragedy of the sixteenth and seventeenth centuries that the period saw an upsurge in the persecution of witches; in this the Catholic Church played a considerable part. Wherever Reformation and Counter Reformation clashed, fear and ignorance provoked an outcry against witches. This was especially true of those areas which the Protestants sought to convert after about 1560, and of those areas reconquered by the Catholics in the 1580s, 1590s and 1620s. Where Protestant or Catholic authority found itself stubbornly resisted it often identified opposition with some form of witchcraft. Most leading Catholics, including men like Canisius, accepted the whole witch mythology which was built on the confession of impressionable young girls and elderly women, sometimes under the pressure of torture.

Jesuits like del Rio, and German bishops such as Philipp Adolf von Ehrenberg of Würzburg and a great many of his contemporaries, urged on the persecution. Bavaria and other parts of south Germany, the Rhineland, Poland, Flanders and south-east Europe were all terribly affected between 1580 and 1648. In Würzburg alone, Archbishop Philipp Adoff reckoned to have executed 900 people including his own nephew, nineteen priests and even children under seven, during his eight years in office. The Catholic Church was no more guilty in this than the Protestants, but this cannot reduce the tragedy of a situation brought on by hostility and fear. Where religious strife was less, as in Spain, so persecution of witches was itself proportionally smaller.

By the middle of the seventeenth century the burst of energy and the deep spirituality released by the Counter Reformation had largely run its course, but to have lasted for over a century was itself a major achievement. The Church took many wrong turnings and always sought refuge in discipline and order, orthodoxy and uniformity; thus flexibility and comprehensiveness were sacrificed as the medieval Church was transformed to meet the challenges of the sixteenth and seventeenth centuries.

The discipline and, above all, the administrative efficiency which made that discipline enforceable was new and well suited to the spirit of the sixteenth century, yet it created as many problems as it solved. None of this, however, should obscure the great achievements. Bigotry, oppression and dull conformity were only one side of the picture. Gentleness, love, charity and religious energy were also present and the Church once more offered to the mass of peasantry a message of hope; through its symbols and its rituals it produced a peace and a security which the world could not provide.

Appendix I

THE POPES OF THE LATE MEDIEVAL AND EARLY MODERN PERIOD

1417–31	Martin V	(Colonna)
1431–47	Eugenius IV	(Condulmaro)
1447–55	Nicholas V	(Thomas of Sarzana)
1455–8	Calixtus III	(Borgia)
1458–64	Pius II	(Piccolomini)
1464–71	Paul II	(Barbo)
1471–84	Sixtus IV	(della Rovere)
1484–92	Innocent VIII	(Cibo)
1492–1503	Alexander VI	(Borgia)
1503	Pius III	(Todeschini)
1503–13	Julius II	(della Rovere)
1513–21	Leo X	(Medici)
1522–3	Adrian VI	(Adrian of Utrecht)
1523–34	Clement VII	(Medici)
1534–49	Paul III	(Farnese)
1550–5	Julius III	(del Monte)
1555	Marcellus II	(Cervini)
1555–9	Paul IV	(Carafa)
1559–65	Pius IV	(Medici)
1566–72	Pius V	(Ghislieri)
1572–85	Gregory XIII	(Buoncompagno)
1585–90	Sixtus V	(Peretti)
1590	Urban VII	(Castagna)
1590–1	Gregory XIV	(Sfondrato)
1591	Innocent IX	(Fachinetto)
1592–1605	Clement VIII	(Aldobrandini)
1605	Leo XI	(Medici)
1605–21	Paul V	(Borghese)
1621–3	Gregory XV	(Ludovisi)
1623–44	Urban VIII	(Barberini)
1644–55	Innocent X	(Pamfili)

Appendix II

THE SECULAR RULERS

England
1485–1509	Henry VII
1509–47	Henry VIII
1547–53	Edward VI
1553–8	Mary
1558–1603	Elizabeth
1603–25	James I
1625–49	Charles I
[1649–60	Interregnum]
1660–85	Charles II
1685–8	James II

France
1461–83	Louis XI
1483–98	Charles VIII
1498–1515	Louis XII
1515–47	Francis I
1547–59	Henry II
1559–60	Francis II
1560–74	Charles IX
1574–89	Henry III
1589–1610	Henry IV
1610–43	Louis XIII
1643–1715	Louis XIV

Spain
1479–1516	Ferdinand (and, until 1504, Isabella)
1516–58	Charles I
1558–98	Philip II
1598–1621	Philip III
1621–65	Philip IV
1665–1700	Charles II

The Holy Roman Empire
1493–1519	Maximillian I
1519–56	Charles V
1556–64	Ferdinand I
1564–76	Maximillian II
1576–1612	Rudolph II
1612–19	Matthias
1619–37	Ferdinand II
1637–57	Ferdinand III
1657–1705	Leopold I

Poland
1506–48	Sigismund I
1548–72	Sigismund II Augustus
1572–6	Henry of Valois
1576–86	Stephen Bathory
1587–1632	Sigismund III

The early Generals of the Jesuit Society
1540–56   Loyola
1556–64   Lainez
1565–72   Borgia
1573–81   Mercurian
1581–1615 Aquaviva

Appendix III

GENEALOGICAL TABLES

The Spanish and Austrian Hapsburgs

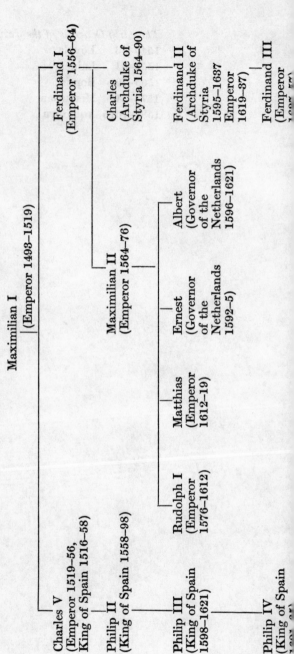

Maximilian I
(Emperor 1493–1519)

Charles V
(Emperor 1519–56,
King of Spain 1516–58)

Ferdinand I
(Emperor 1556–64)

Philip II
(King of Spain 1558–98)

Maximilian II
(Emperor 1564–76)

Charles
(Archduke of
Styria 1564–90)

Rudolph I
(Emperor
1576–1612)

Matthias
(Emperor
1612–19)

Ernest
(Governor
of the
Netherlands
1592–5)

Albert
(Governor
of the
Netherlands
1596–1621)

Ferdinand II
(Archduke of
Styria
1595–1637
Emperor
1619–37)

Philip III
(King of Spain
1598–1621)

Philip IV
(King of Spain
1621–65)

Ferdinand III
(Emperor
1637–57)

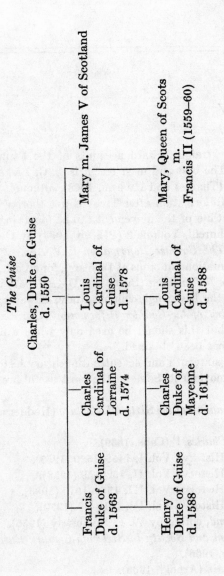

The Guise

Charles, Duke of Guise
d. 1550

	Louis	Mary m. James V of Scotland
	Cardinal of Guise	
	d. 1578	

Francis
Duke of Guise
d. 1563

Charles
Cardinal of Lorraine
d. 1574

Louis
Cardinal of Guise
d. 1588

Henry
Duke of Guise
d. 1588

Charles
Duke of Mayenne
d. 1611

Mary, Queen of Scots
m.
Francis II (1559–60)

Appendix IV

BIBLIOGRAPHY

There are few adequate, straightforward accounts of the Counter Reformation in English. The best and most recent is A. G. Dickens, *The Counter Reformation* (Thames and Hudson, 1968), although the progress of the Counter Reformation after Trent is not thoroughly pursued. An excellent outline of the movement can be found in the 'Pelican History of the Church', Volume 3 (Pelican, 1964) by Owen Chadwick; B. J. Kidd, *The Counter Reformation* (S.P.C.K., 1933) contains some useful information but stops at 1600 and, for a Catholic viewpoint P. Hughes, *The Reformation* (Burns and Oates, 1957) is a useful corrective. By far the best single-volume study, however, is H. O. Evennett, *The Spirit of the Counter Reformation* (Cambridge University Press, 1968), but this should be used only when a firm grounding in the subject has been obtained.

Many general works on sixteenth and seventeenth-century history deal with aspects of the movement. Some of the most useful are:

R. H. Bainton, *The Reformation of the Sixteenth Century* (Hodder and Stoughton, 1957).

K. Brandi, *The Emperor Charles V* (Cape, 1939).

'New Cambridge Modern History', Vol. I, 1453–1520 (1957).

'New Cambridge Modern History', Vol. II, 1520–59 (1958).

'New Cambridge Modern History', Vol. III, 1559–1610 (1968).

'New Cambridge Modern History', Vol. IV, 1610–59 (1970).

Cambridge History of Poland, edited by W. F. Reddaway (1950).

A. G. Dickens, *Reformation and Society in Sixteenth-Century Europe* (Thames and Hudson, 1966).

J. H. Elliott, *Imperial Spain* (Arnold, 1963).

J. H. Elliott, *Europe Divided* (Fontana, 1968).

G. R. Elton, *Reformation Europe* (Fontana, 1963).

G. R. Elton, *England under the Tudors* (Methuen, 1955).

P. Geyl, *The Revolt of the Netherlands* (Williams and Norgate, 1932).

P. Geyl, *The Netherlands in the Seventeenth Century*, Parts I and II (Benn, 1964).

D. Hay, *Europe in the Fourteenth and Fifteenth Centuries* (Longmans, 1964).

D. Hay, *The Medieval Centuries* (Methuen, 'University Paperbacks,' 1964).

H. Holborn, *A History of Modern Germany, The Reformation* (Eyre and Spottiswood, 1965).

M. Keen, *Medieval Europe* (Routledge and Kegan Paul, 1968).

H. V. Livermore, *A History of Portugal* (Cambridge University Press, 1947).

J. Lynch, *Spain under the Hapsburgs*, Vols I and II (Blackwell, 1969).

J. E. Neale, *The Age of Catherine de Medici* (Cape, 1943).

M. M. Phillips, *Erasmus and the Northern Renaissance* (English Universities Press, 1949).

S. H. Steinberg, *The Thirty Years' War and the Conflict for European Hegemony* 1600–60 (Arnold, 1966).

G. R. R. Treasure, *Seventeenth-Century France* (Rivingtons, 1966).

H. R. Trevor-Roper, *The Rise of Christian Europe* (Thames and Hudson, 1965).

A number of books are available for a more detailed study of the subject. An outline of the theology of the medieval Church may be found in G. Leff, *Medieval Thought from St Augustine to Occam* (Penguin, 1958) or in M. D. Knowles, *The Evolution of Medieval Thought* (Longmans, 1962), while on the sixteenth century J. W. Allen, *A History of Political Thought in the Sixteenth Century* (Methuen 1941) is the best. For an outline of the political theories of the whole period, including those of the Jesuits, G. H. Sabine, *A History of Political Theory* (Harrap, 1947) is the best. S. Neill, *A History of Christian Missions* (Pelican, 1965) gives an outline of the activities of the Catholic Missionaries overseas, while P. McGrath, *Papists and Puritans under Elizabeth I* (Blandford, 1967) is a full account of the attempts to re-convert England. There are several books on the revival of witchcraft in the period, the most concise being H. R. Trevor-Roper, *The European Witch-Craze of the Sixteenth and Seventeenth Centuries* (Pelican, 1969). *The Borgia Testament* (Collins, 1948) by Nigel Balchin is a novel which catches the atmosphere of Rome in the period of Alexander VI, and illustrates the family

quarrels which surrounded the Papacy. There are several histories of
the Jesuits, one of the more recent being C. Hollis, *The Jesuits*
(Weidenfeld and Nicolson, 1968) – an interesting although not too
detailed study. A most useful collection of essays on the Reformation
is edited by J. Hurstfield under the title *The Reformation Crisis*
(Arnold, 1965); these include a valuable chapter on the Counter
Reformation by H. O. Evennett.

Various periodicals contain articles which examine in depth
specific aspects of the movements. Of these the most useful are:

History Today
July   1962 J. B. Morall, 'The Council of Trent'
November 1970 J. Hook, 'The Counter Reformation in Italy'
July   1971 J. Hook, 'Bernini and Rome'

Past and Present
Number 9 G. Leff, 'The Fourteenth Century and the Decline of
                 Scholasticism'
Number 20 G. Leff, 'Heresy and the Decline of the Church'
Number 21 J. Bossy, 'The Character of Elizabethan Catholicism'
Number 30 M. Aston, 'John Wyclif's Reformation Reputation'
Number 47 J. Bossy, 'The Counter Reformation and the People of
                 Catholic Europe'

Index

Dates indicate life-span except in the case of popes and secular rulers where they signify the period of rule.

Acarie, Madame (1566–1618), 153–4

Adrian VI (1522–3), 14, 47, 72

Albert V, Duke of Bavaria (1550–79), 134, 135, 142

Albert, Archduke, Ruler of the Spanish Netherlands (1596–1621), 121–2

Alexander VI (1492–1503), 15, 43, 51–2

Allen, Cardinal William (1532–94), 126–7, 128,129

Alva, Duke of (1507–82), 116, 120

Anabaptism, 9, 18, 26, 103, 119, 140

Aquinas, St Thomas (1226–74), 9, 20–1, 29

Armada, the Spanish (1588), 118, 127, 129, 166

Augustinianism, 19, 21, 75, 84, 155

Austria (including Styria), 45, 79, 90, 105, 106, 139, 140–3, 144, 166, 167, 168

Avignon Captivity (1309–79), 12–13, 14, 26, 31, 35

Barnabites, the 59, 74

Baroque Art, 172–5

Bathory, Stephen, King of Poland (1576–86), 146, 148, 149

Bavaria, 30, 106, 107, 134, 135–6, 137, 138, 140, 142, 144, 160, 168, 175

Bellarmine, Robert (1542–1621), 151, 171

Benedictine Order, 18, 40, 48, 154

Bernini, Lorenzo (1598–1680), 107, 174–5

Bérulle, Pierre de (1575–1629), 153

Bohemia (including Lusatia, Moravia and Silesia), 31, 33–5, 36, 107, 140, 143–4, 167

Boniface VIII (1294–1303), 11, 12, 13

Borromeo, Carlo (1538–84), 16, 92, 93, 102, 103, 104, 105, 116, 132, 169

Brandenburg, 16, 24, 138

Brethren of the Common Life, 40, 67, 70

Bull of Excommunication (1570), 126–7

Calixtus III (1455–8), 50

Calvin, John (1509–64), 23, 48, 61, 76, 95

Calvinsim, 26, 35, 92, 114, 115, 119, 120, 132, 134, 140, 144, 146, 151, 152, 154, 167, 172

Campion, Edmund (1540–81), 128–9

Canisius, Peter (1521–97), 134–5, 142, 175

Capucin Order, 59, 77, 132, 151

Carafa, Gian Pietro, Paul IV (1555–9), 57, 58, 59, 73, 76, 77, 78, 79, 91–2, 104, 124, 172

Caraveggio, Michelangelo de (1565–1610), 173–4

Carmelite Order, 19

Carmelites, Discaled, 117

Carranza, Bartolomé (1503–76), 116

Carthusian Order, 18, 66

Catherine of Genoa (1447–1510), 57

Catherine de Medici (1519–89), 92

Cervini, Marcello, Marcellus II (1555), 73, 81, 87, 91

Charles V, King of Spain (1516–58), Emperor (1519–56), 8, 45, 47, 70, 71, 72, 73, 77, 78, 79, 81, 82, 85–7, 89, 90, 113, 119

Charles IX, King of France (1560–74), 99

Charles, Archduke of Styria
(1564–90), 142
Cistercian Order, 18
Clement V (1303–14), 12
Clement VII (1523–34), 58, 72–3
Clement VIII (1592–1605), 101, 106,
142, 152
Cochlaeus, John (1478–1552), 26, 70
Colet, John (1467–1519), 69, 70
Cologne Dispute (1582–5), 136–7
Conciliar Movement, 35–9, 52,
55–6, 81, 95
Congregation for the Propagation
of the Faith, 105, 106, 107, 159
Congregation of Clerks Regular,
see Theatines
Consilium de Emendenda Ecclesia
(1537), 74–5
Contarini, Gaspar (1483–1542), 58,
62, 68, 73, 74, 75, 76, 77, 103
Councils
Pisa (1409), 13, 36
Constance (1414–18), 13, 32, 34,
36–7
Pavia/Siena (1423–4), 37–8
Basle/ Ferrara/Florence/Rome
(1431–47), 38
Fifth Lateran (1512–17), 52–3, 56
Trent (1545–63), 71, 79, 81–96,
99, 100, 102, 103, 104, 105, 106,
107, 108, 115, 118, 120, 132,
137, 138, 146, 147, 148, 151,
152, 165, 167, 168, 169, 172
Cromwell, Thomas (1485–1540), 8,
19, 30, 44, 69

Dataria, the, 88, 91, 104
del Monte, Gian Maria, Julius III
(1550–5), 81, 88, 91
Denmark, 150
Dominican Order, 19, 84, 94, 101,
115, 119, 154, 155, 165
Donation of Constantine, 11–12, 44
Douai, College of, 126, 127, 128

Eck, John (1486–1543), 26, 56, 70,
132
El Greco (1541–1614), 173

Elizabeth I, Queen of England
(1558–1603), 99, 124, 125, 126,
127, 128, 130, 165
England, 8, 9, 10, 12, 15, 17, 19, 30,
31–2, 36, 37, 44–5, 66, 68, 69, 72,
88, 92, 99, 101, 123–30, 165, 170,
172
Erasmus, Desiderius (1466–1536),
19, 26, 41, 48, 67–9, 70, 75, 78, 87,
113, 114, 115
Ernest, Prince of Bavaria (1583–
1612), 136, 137, 138
Eugenius IV (1431–47), 38, 50

Felix, V, pretended pope (1439–49),
38
Ferdinand of Aragon, King of
Spain (1479–1516), 39, 46–7, 113,
156
Ferdinand I, Emperor (1556–64),
90, 92, 93, 133, 134
Ferdinand II (of Styria), Emperor
(1619–37), 107, 139, 140, 142–5,
150, 160, 166
Feuillant Order, 151, 154
Fisher, John (1459–1535), 16, 68,
69, 73, 87
France, 8, 10, 12, 13, 15, 36, 37, 45,
52, 60, 67, 69–70, 71, 72, 89, 92,
93, 96, 99, 101, 103, 105, 107, 114,
115, 123, 146, 150–6, 158, 167,
168, 171, 172
Francis I, King of France (1515–47),
8, 45, 69, 71, 77, 78, 81, 85, 151
Francis de Sales (1567–1622), 132,
154
Franciscan Order, 19, 40, 42, 148,
153, 154
see also Observant Franciscans

Galileo Galilei (1564–1642), 170
Germany, 8, 9, 12, 15, 16, 18, 23, 30,
33, 37, 44, 45, 55–6, 59, 61, 69,
70–3, 76, 85–6, 87, 89, 90, 91, 92,
96, 113, 114, 132–40, 143, 165,
167, 168, 170,175
Giberti, Gian Matteo (1495–1543),
58, 66

Giles of Rome (1247–1316), 9, 11
Gregory VII (1073–85), 11, 15, 35
Gregory XIII (1572–85), 100, 105,
    106, 128, 134, 142
Gregory XV (1621–3), 107, 159
Gropper, Johannes (1503–59), 76,
    77
Guise, Charles de, Cardinal of
    Lorraine (1525–74), 89, 93, 151
Gunpowder Plot (1605), 130

Henry VII, King of England
    (1485–1509), 8, 44–5
Henry VIII, King of England
    (1509–47), 8, 45, 52, 68, 69, 78, 123
Henry II, King of France (1547–59),
    89, 91, 150, 151
Henry IV, King of France
    (1589–1610), 101, 150
Henry I, King of Portugal
    (1578–80), 131
Hosius, Stanislaus (1504–79),
    147–8, 149, 150
Hungary, 144–5
Huss, John (1369–1415), 31, 32,
    33–5, 40
Hussitism, 33–5, 36, 50, 140, 167

Illuminism, 113–14, 115
Index, the, 78, 83, 95, 100, 101, 103,
    106, 170
Innocent III (1198–1216), 11, 12,
    13, 14, 15
Innocent IV (1243–54), 12
Innocent VIII (1485–92), 51
Innocent X (1644–55), 107
Inquisition, the Roman, 69, 77–8,
    91, 99, 101, 103, 104, 105, 106, 170
Inquisition, the Spanish, 47, 49, 61,
    77, 102, 113, 114, 115, 116, 119
Ireland, 128, 130, 167
Isabella of Castile, Queen of Spain
    (1479–1504), 39, 47–9, 113, 156
Isabella, Archduchess of the
    Spanish Netherlands (1566–1633),
    121
Italy, 7, 8, 9, 15, 23, 38, 42–3, 45,
    50–3, 56, 57–60, 62, 66, 72–4, 78,

81, 87, 103–4, 105, 106, 107, 123,
    152, 165, 166, 170, 172, 173, 174,
    175

James I, King of England (1603–25),
    127, 130
Jansenism, 155
Jesus, Society of, 60–4, 65, 74, 84,
    94, 100, 101, 103–4, 106, 108,
    115, 118, 119, 122, 128–9, 131–2,
    134–5, 137, 138, 139, 140, 142, 143,
    144, 145, 147–8, 149, 150, 151,
    152, 154–5, 156, 157, 158, 159–60,
    165, 166, 168–9, 171–2, 174, 175
John III, King of Portugal
    (1521–57), 131, 156
John III, King of Sweden (1568–92),
    150
John of Paris (d. 1306), 9, 12
St John of God (1485–1550), 117
Julius II (1503–13), 15, 47, 52
Julius III, see del Monte

Lainez, Diego (1512–65), 62, 64, 91,
    159
Laski, John (d. 1531), 72, 147
Lazarists, 153
League, Roman Catholic (1609),
    138–9
Leo X (1513–21), 24, 52–3, 69
Lepanto, the Battle of (1571), 100,
    102, 116
Louis XIII, King of France
    (1610–43), 152
Louis XIV, King of France
    (1643–1715), 152, 155, 156
Loyola, Ignatius (1491–1556),
    60–2, 63, 64, 65, 74, 91, 134, 159,
    160, 166, 172
Luiz de Leon (1528–91), 118
Luther, Martin (1483–1546), 16, 23,
    24, 29, 31, 34, 45, 48, 53, 55–6,
    60, 69, 70, 71, 74, 76, 77, 83, 84,
    85, 88, 95, 132, 134, 147
Lutheranism, 8, 26, 56, 70, 71, 72,
    74, 76, 82, 83, 86, 92, 113, 115,
    119, 132, 133, 139, 140, 142, 144,
    146, 147, 150, 151, 166, 169

Marcellus II, *see* Cervini

Marsilio of Padua (1270–1342), 9, 29, 30, 35

Martin V (1417–31), 13, 34, 37, 50

Mary, Queen of England (1553–8), 123–4

Mary, Queen of Scots (1542–87), 99, 127, 130

Massacre of St Bartholomew's Day (1572), 146

Matthias, Emperor (1612–19), 143

Maximilian II, Emperor (1564–76), 93, 133, 140

Maximilian, Duke of Bavaria (1597–1651), 107, 135, 138–9, 144, 160, 166

More, Thomas (1478–1535), 26, 68, 69, 87

Morone, Giovanni (1509–80), 73, 92, 93, 94, 95, 103

Morisco, Revolt of (1567), 114

Muhlberg, Battle of (1547), 86

Nantes, Edict of (1598), 152, 156

Neri, Philip (1515–95), 59–60

Netherlands, the (including the United Provinces), 7, 9, 10, 23, 40–1, 99, 106, 114, 115, 119–23, 125, 129, 166, 167, 168, 170, 172, 175

Nicholas V (1447–55), 50

Nicholas of Cusa (1400–64), 41, 42

Northern Rebellion, the (1569), 127

Observant Franciscan Order, 42, 48, 66

Oratory of the Divine Love, 57–8, 59, 74

Palatinate, the, 107, 134, 138. 139, 140

Palestrina, Giovanni (1526–94), 172

Papal Administration, 13–15, 51, 100–1, 104–6, 107, 168–9

Papal States, the, 15, 52, 100, 102, 104, 105

Parma, Duke of (1545–92), 120–1

Parsons, Nicholas (1546–1610), 127, 128, 129

Paul II (1464–71), 51

Paul III (1534–49), 39, 62, 71, 73–9, 81, 85–7, 88

Paul IV, *see* Carafa

Paul V (1605–21), 106

Philip II, King of Spain (1558–98), 93, 95, 96, 99, 101, 102, 113, 114, 115, 116, 117, 119, 120, 123, 124, 127, 140, 166

Pius II (1458–64), 38, 39, 50

Pius IV (1559–65), 92, 93, 95, 104, 105, 116

Pius V (1566–72), 99–100, 105, 116, 120, 127

Poland, 72, 101, 105, 131–2, 146–50, 160, 165, 166, 167, 175

Pole, Reginald (1500–58), 73, 81, 82, 87, 88, 96, 123–4

Portugal, 10, 15, 59, 96, 128, 156

Quiroga, Caspar de (1512–94), 116, 117, 118

Regensburg, Diet of (1541), 76–7

Renaissance, the, 9, 15, 42, 43–4, 50, 51, 52, 103, 106, 170, 173

Requesens, Don Luis de (1528–76), 102, 120

Restitution, Edict of (1629), 139, 140

Reuchlin, John (1455–1522), 70

Ricci, Matthew (1522–1610), 157–8

Richelieu, Cardinal (1585–1642), 152–3

Robert de Nobili (1577–1656), 157

Rubens, Peter Paul (1577–1640), 123, 174

Rudolph II, Emperor (1576–1612), 134, 135, 136, 142, 143, 145, 160, 166

Sack of Rome, the (1527), 66, 73

Sadoleto, Jacopo (1477–1547), 58, 66, 73

Sanders, Nicholas (1530–81), 127, 128

Savonarola (1452–98), 42–3, 46, 57

Saxony, 85, 138, 144

Schism, the Great (1378–1417), 13, 26, 31, 35, 36, 37, 53

Schmalkaldic League, the, 86

Scotland, 101, 130–1, 170

Sigismund I, King of Poland (1506–48), 72, 146

Sigismund II Augustus, King of Poland (1548–72), 146

Sigismund III, King of Poland (1586–1632), 146, 148, 149, 150, 166

Sixtus IV (1471–84), 51

Sixtus V (1585–90), 100–1, 105

Sommaschi, the, 59

Spain, 7, 8, 10, 15, 37, 39, 42, 44, 46–50, 53, 56, 57, 59, 60, 61, 66, 70, 72, 91, 93, 96, 100–1, 102, 105, 113–23, 127, 128, 129, 135, 139, 151, 152, 153, 154, 158, 166, 168, 170, 175

Stukeley, Thomas (1525–78), 128

Styria, see Austria

Suarez, Francisco de (1548–1617), 171

Sweden, 8, 41, 44, 139, 140, 146, 149–50

Switzerland, 67, 96, 132, 135

Teresa de Avila (1515–82), 116–17, 118, 166

Theatines, the, 58–9

Thomas à Kempis (1379–1471), 41, 60–1, 117

Tomicki, Peter (d. 1535), 72, 147

Transubstantiation, 21, 77, 89–90

treaties and agreements
Augsburg (1555), 90, 133, 136, 137, 139
Bologna, Concordat of (1516), 8, 45, 69, 151
Bourges, Pragmatic Sanction of (1438), 8, 45
Cateau Cambrèsis (1559), 91
Crèpy (1544), 71, 79, 85
Interim of Augsburg (1548), 86
Letters of Majesty (1609), 143
Prague (1635), 140
Westphalia (1648), 139, 140

United Provinces, the, see the Netherlands

Urban VIII (1623–44), 107, 174

Ursuline Order, 59, 74, 158

Valdes, Juan de (1483–1568), 114, 116

Valla, Lorenzo (1406–64), 12, 44

St Vincent de Paul (1576–1660), 152, 153–4

Vittoria, Tommasso (1540–1611), 172

Waldensians, the, 35

Wallenstein, Albrecht von (1583–1634), 139

White Mountain, Battle of (1620), 144

William V, Duke of Bavaria (1579–97), 135

William of Occam (1300–49), 9, 20, 29–30, 32, 35

Wolsey, Thomas (1475–1530), 14, 15, 16, 69

Worms, Diet of (1520), 34

Wyclif, John (1320–84), 30–2, 35, 40

Xavier, Francis (1506–52), 62, 131–2, 156–7

Ximenes, Cardinal (1436–1517), 16, 42, 48, 66

Zwinglianism, 35